The Federal Trade Commission

The Federal Trade Commission

Pamela B. Stuart

CHELSEA HOUSE PUBLISHERS

On the cover: FTC staff members discuss a pending case.
Frontispiece: An aerial view of the Federal Triangle, with the Federal Trade Commission building in the foreground.

Chelsea House Publishers
Editor-in-Chief: Remmel Nunn
Managing Editor: Karyn Gullen Browne
Copy Chief: Juliann Barbato
Picture Editor: Adrian G. Allen
Art Director: Maria Epes
Deputy Copy Chief: Mark Rifkin
Assistant Art Director: Noreen Romano
Manufacturing Manager: Gerald Levine
Systems Manager: Lindsey Ottman
Production Manager: Joseph Romano
Production Coordinator: Marie Claire Cebrián

Know Your Government
Senior Editor: Kathy Kuhtz

Staff for THE FEDERAL TRADE COMMISSION
Associate Editor: Scott Prentzas
Copy Editor: Brian Sookram
Picture Researcher: Melanie Sanford

First Printing

1   3   5   7   9   8   6   4   2   *92-18482*

Library of Congress Cataloging in Publication Data

Stuart, Pamela B.
   The Federal Trade Commission / Pamela B. Stuart.
      p.   cm.—(Know your government)
   Includes bibliographical references and index.
   ISBN 1-55546-114-X
   1. United States. Federal Trade Commission   2. Industry and state—United
States.   3. Trade regulation—United States.   I. Title.   II. Series: Know your govern-
ment (New York, NY)
HD3616.U47S77   1991   90-20519
353.0082′6—dc20   CIP

52174

CONTENTS

KNOW YOUR GOVERNMENT

CHELSEA HOUSE PUBLISHERS

INTRODUCTION

Government: Crises of Confidence

Arthur M. Schlesinger, jr.

From the start, Americans have regarded their government with a mixture of reliance and mistrust. The men who founded the republic did not doubt the indispensability of government. "If men were angels," observed the 51st Federalist Paper, "no government would be necessary." But men are not angels. Because human beings are subject to wicked as well as to noble impulses, government was deemed essential to assure freedom and order.

At the same time, the American revolutionaries knew that government could also become a source of injury and oppression. The men who gathered in Philadelphia in 1787 to write the Constitution therefore had two purposes in mind. They wanted to establish a strong central authority and to limit that central authority's capacity to abuse its power.

To prevent the abuse of power, the Founding Fathers wrote two basic principles into the new Constitution. The principle of federalism divided power between the state governments and the central authority. The principle of the separation of powers subdivided the central authority itself into three branches—the executive, the legislative, and the judiciary—so that "each may be a check on the other." The *Know Your Government* series focuses on the major executive departments and agencies in these branches of the federal government.

The Constitution did not plan the executive branch in any detail. After vesting the executive power in the president, it assumed the existence of "executive departments" without specifying what these departments should be. Congress began defining their functions in 1789 by creating the Departments of State, Treasury, and War. The secretaries in charge of these departments made up President Washington's first cabinet. Congress also provided for a legal officer, and President Washington soon invited the attorney general, as he was called, to attend cabinet meetings. As need required, Congress created more executive departments.

Setting up the cabinet was only the first step in organizing the American state. With almost no guidance from the Constitution, President Washington, seconded by Alexander Hamilton, his brilliant secretary of the treasury, equipped the infant republic with a working administrative structure. The Federalists believed in both executive energy and executive accountability and set high standards for public appointments. The Jeffersonian opposition had less faith in strong government and preferred local government to the central authority. But when Jefferson himself became president in 1801, although he set out to change the direction of policy, he found no reason to alter the framework the Federalists had erected.

By 1801 there were about 3,000 federal civilian employees in a nation of a little more than 5 million people. Growth in territory and population steadily enlarged national responsibilities. Thirty years later, when Jackson was president, there were more than 11,000 government workers in a nation of 13 million. The federal establishment was increasing at a faster rate than the population.

Jackson's presidency brought significant changes in the federal service. He believed that the executive branch contained too many officials who saw their jobs as "species of property" and as "a means of promoting individual interest." Against the idea of a permanent service based on life tenure, Jackson argued for the periodic redistribution of federal offices, contending that this was the democratic way and that official duties could be made "so plain and simple that men of intelligence may readily qualify themselves for their performance." He called this policy rotation-in-office. His opponents called it the spoils system.

In fact, partisan legend exaggerated the extent of Jackson's removals. More than 80 percent of federal officeholders retained their jobs. Jackson discharged no larger a proportion of government workers than Jefferson had done a generation earlier. But the rise in these years of mass political parties gave federal patronage new importance as a means of building the party and of rewarding activists. Jackson's successors were less restrained in the distribu-

8

tion of spoils. As the federal establishment grew—to nearly 40,000 by 1861—the politicization of the public service excited increasing concern.

After the Civil War the spoils system became a major political issue. High-minded men condemned it as the root of all political evil. The spoilsmen, said the British commentator James Bryce, "have distorted and depraved the mechanism of politics." Patronage, by giving jobs to unqualified, incompetent, and dishonest persons, lowered the standards of public service and nourished corrupt political machines. Office-seekers pursued presidents and cabinet secretaries without mercy. "Patronage," said Ulysses S. Grant after his presidency, "is the bane of the presidential office." "Every time I appoint someone to office," said another political leader, "I make a hundred enemies and one ingrate." George William Curtis, the president of the National Civil Service Reform League, summed up the indictment. He said,

> The theory which perverts public trusts into party spoils, making public employment dependent upon personal favor and not on proved merit, necessarily ruins the self-respect of public employees, destroys the function of party in a republic, prostitutes elections into a desperate strife for personal profit, and degrades the national character by lowering the moral tone and standard of the country.

The object of civil service reform was to promote efficiency and honesty in the public service and to bring about the ethical regeneration of public life. Over bitter opposition from politicians, the reformers in 1883 passed the Pendleton Act, establishing a bipartisan Civil Service Commission, competitive examinations, and appointment on merit. The Pendleton Act also gave the president authority to extend by executive order the number of "classified" jobs—that is, jobs subject to the merit system. The act applied initially only to about 14,000 of the more than 100,000 federal positions. But by the end of the 19th century 40 percent of federal jobs had moved into the classified category.

Civil service reform was in part a response to the growing complexity of American life. As society grew more organized and problems more technical, official duties were no longer so plain and simple that any person of intelligence could perform them. In public service, as in other areas, the all-round man was yielding ground to the expert, the amateur to the professional. The excesses of the spoils system thus provoked the counter-ideal of scientific public administration, separate from politics and, as far as possible, insulated against it.

The cult of the expert, however, had its own excesses. The idea that administration could be divorced from policy was an illusion. And in the realm of policy, the expert, however much segregated from partisan politics, can never attain perfect objectivity. He remains the prisoner of his own set of values. It is these values rather than technical expertise that determine fundamental judgments of public policy. To turn over such judgments to experts, moreover, would be to abandon democracy itself; for in a democracy final decisions must be made by the people and their elected representatives. "The business of the expert," the British political scientist Harold Laski rightly said, "is to be on tap and not on top."

Politics, however, were deeply ingrained in American folkways. This meant intermittent tension between the presidential government, elected every four years by the people, and the permanent government, which saw presidents come and go while it went on forever. Sometimes the permanent government knew better than its political masters; sometimes it opposed or sabotaged valuable new initiatives. In the end a strong president with effective cabinet secretaries could make the permanent government responsive to presidential purpose, but it was often an exasperating struggle.

The struggle within the executive branch was less important, however, than the growing impatience with bureaucracy in society as a whole. The 20th century saw a considerable expansion of the federal establishment. The Great Depression and the New Deal led the national government to take on a variety of new responsibilities. The New Deal extended the federal regulatory apparatus. By 1940, in a nation of 130 million people, the number of federal workers for the first time passed the 1 million mark. The Second World War brought federal civilian employment to 3.8 million in 1945. With peace, the federal establishment declined to around 2 million by 1950. Then growth resumed, reaching 2.8 million by the 1980s.

The New Deal years saw rising criticism of "big government" and "bureaucracy." Businessmen resented federal regulation. Conservatives worried about the impact of paternalistic government on individual self-reliance, on community responsibility, and on economic and personal freedom. The nation in effect renewed the old debate between Hamilton and Jefferson in the early republic, although with an ironic exchange of positions. For the Hamiltonian constituency, the "rich and well-born," once the advocate of affirmative government, now condemned government intervention, while the Jeffersonian constituency, the plain people, once the advocate of a weak central government and of states' rights, now favored government intervention.

In the 1980s, with the presidency of Ronald Reagan, the debate has burst out with unusual intensity. According to conservatives, government intervention abridges liberty, stifles enterprise, and is inefficient, wasteful, and arbitrary. It disturbs the harmony of the self-adjusting market and creates worse troubles than it solves. Get government off our backs, according to the popular cliché, and our problems will solve themselves. When government is necessary, let it be at the local level, close to the people. Above all, stop the inexorable growth of the federal government.

In fact, for all the talk about the "swollen" and "bloated" bureaucracy, the federal establishment has not been growing as inexorably as many Americans seem to believe. In 1949, it consisted of 2.1 million people. Thirty years later, while the country had grown by 70 million, the federal force had grown only by 750,000. Federal workers were a smaller percentage of the population in 1985 than they were in 1955—or in 1940. The federal establishment, in short, has not kept pace with population growth. Moreover, national defense and the postal service account for 60 percent of federal employment.

Why then the widespread idea about the remorseless growth of government? It is partly because in the 1960s the national government assumed new and intrusive functions: affirmative action in civil rights, environmental protection, safety and health in the workplace, community organization, legal aid to the poor. Although this enlargement of the federal regulatory role was accompanied by marked growth in the size of government on all levels, the expansion has taken place primarily in state and local government. Whereas the federal force increased by only 27 percent in the 30 years after 1950, the state and local government force increased by an astonishing 212 percent.

Despite the statistics, the conviction flourishes in some minds that the national government is a steadily growing behemoth swallowing up the liberties of the people. The foes of Washington prefer local government, feeling it is closer to the people and therefore allegedly more responsive to popular needs. Obviously there is a great deal to be said for settling local questions locally. But local government is characteristically the government of the locally powerful. Historically, the way the locally powerless have won their human and constitutional rights has often been through appeal to the national government. The national government has vindicated racial justice against local bigotry, defended the Bill of Rights against local vigilantism, and protected natural resources against local greed. It has civilized industry and secured the rights of labor organizations. Had the states' rights creed prevailed, there would perhaps still be slavery in the United States.

The national authority, far from diminishing the individual, has given most Americans more personal dignity and liberty than ever before. The individual freedoms destroyed by the increase in national authority have been in the main the freedom to deny black Americans their rights as citizens; the freedom to put small children to work in mills and immigrants in sweatshops; the freedom to pay starvation wages, require barbarous working hours, and permit squalid working conditions; the freedom to deceive in the sale of goods and securities; the freedom to pollute the environment—all freedoms that, one supposes, a civilized nation can readily do without.

"Statements are made," said President John F. Kennedy in 1963, "labelling the Federal Government an outsider, an intruder, an adversary. . . . The United States Government is not a stranger or not an enemy. It is the people of fifty states joining in a national effort. . . . Only a great national effort by a great people working together can explore the mysteries of space, harvest the products at the bottom of the ocean, and mobilize the human, natural, and material resources of our lands."

So an old debate continues. However, Americans are of two minds. When pollsters ask large, spacious questions—Do you think government has become too involved in your lives? Do you think government should stop regulating business?—a sizable majority opposes big government. But when asked specific questions about the practical work of government—Do you favor social security? unemployment compensation? Medicare? health and safety standards in factories? environmental protection? government guarantee of jobs for everyone seeking employment? price and wage controls when inflation threatens?—a sizable majority approves of intervention.

In general, Americans do not want less government. What they want is more efficient government. They want government to do a better job. For a time in the 1970s, with Vietnam and Watergate, Americans lost confidence in the national government. In 1964, more than three-quarters of those polled had thought the national government could be trusted to do right most of the time. By 1980 only one-quarter was prepared to offer such trust. But by 1984 trust in the federal government to manage national affairs had climbed back to 45 percent.

Bureaucracy is a term of abuse. But it is impossible to run any large organization, whether public or private, without a bureaucracy's division of labor and hierarchy of authority. And we live in a world of large organizations. Without bureaucracy modern society would collapse. The problem is not to abolish bureaucracy, but to make it flexible, efficient, and capable of innovation.

Two hundred years after the drafting of the Constitution, Americans still regard government with a mixture of reliance and mistrust—a good combination. Mistrust is the best way to keep government reliable. Informed criticism is the means of correcting governmental inefficiency, incompetence, and arbitrariness; that is, of best enabling government to play its essential role. For without government, we cannot attain the goals of the Founding Fathers. Without an understanding of government, we cannot have the informed criticism that makes government do the job right. It is the duty of every American citizen to know our government—which is what this series is all about.

The Federal Trade Commission building, located at the eastern corner of the Federal Triangle in downtown Washington, D.C., houses the FTC staff. The FTC, an independent regulatory agency, protects the free-enterprise system from anticompetitive monopolies and from restraints of trade by helping to enforce federal antitrust laws and protecting consumers from deceptive marketing practices.

ONE

Freedom of Enterprise

From the time of its founding in 1914 as one of the first independent regulatory agencies until its present status as an agency awaiting its own rebirth, the Federal Trade Commission (FTC) has been controversial. At various times it has been called a "king-sized cancer on our economy," a "hectoring, tyrannical and . . . tireless snooper," a "rogue agency gone insane," the National Nanny, and the Little Old Lady of Pennsylvania Avenue. Such condemnation has been directed at the FTC because Congress gave it broad legal power to regulate many of the activities of almost all businesses in the United States. The FTC has consistently been at the center of a tug-of-war among Congress, business interests, and consumers. Occasionally, presidents have entered the fray either to prod the commission into action or to rein in its perceived excesses. Throughout most of its history, the FTC has vacillated between periods when it was criticized for being inactive and periods when the commission's aggressiveness led Congress to reduce its appropriations and powers.

The FTC was founded with the objective of making economic life fairer and more competitive as part of the battle to break the trusts that had come to dominate significant parts of the U.S. economy in the latter half of the 19th century. The roots of the antimonopolist movement in the United States that led to the creation of the FTC stretch as far back as the founding of the nation.

The American Revolution, at its core, was a demand by the colonists for government by the consent of the governed and a protest against centralized power and special privilege. While the colonists sought emancipation from the arbitrary power of King George III, they also sought freedom of enterprise.

The free market, which had been an integral part of the nation's economy since the American Revolution, had been severely constricted by powerful corporations that entered into trust agreements in the second half of the 19th century that enabled them to control all aspects of their business, from the acquisition of raw materials to the ultimate sale of finished products and services to consumers. Many of these organizations—beginning with the railroad pools of the 1870s, the Standard Oil Company of Ohio in 1882, and later the Whiskey Trust, Sugar Trust, Lead Trust, and Cotton-Oil Trust—so dominated their industries that they could control markets and prices without worrying about what competitors might do. The abuses of the trusts caused a resurgence of antimonopolist sentiment and led to the passage of the first antitrust law, the Sherman Antitrust Act, in 1890.

An 1889 cartoon satirizes the power of trusts—companies in the same industry that join together for the purpose of reducing competition and fixing prices—over the federal government. Throughout history, many businesspeople have sought to enhance their status or wealth by monopolizing the market for their products through restrictions on or elimination of competition. The FTC was created in 1914 to prevent such unfair methods of competition in commerce.

During the Progressive era—the period between the beginning of Theodore Roosevelt's presidency in 1901 and the end of World War I in 1918—the public clamored for reforms in politics, business, and social affairs. Whereas the preceding generation had tamed the frontier, settled the continent, and created industrial might, the Progressives sought to reform the most serious abuses of corrupt machine politics and big business. The failure of the Sherman Antitrust Act, as initially interpreted by the federal courts, to thwart the abuses of the trusts led to the drive to establish a regulatory agency that would effectively curb unfair methods of competition. In response to public outcry, Congress passed the Federal Trade Commission Act (FTC Act) and the Clayton Act in 1914. The FTC Act established the FTC and empowered it to prohibit unfair methods of competition and thereby assist the Department of Justice in enforcing the antitrust laws.

In its first decade, the FTC disappointed many of its early supporters because it made little progress in preventing unfair competition and deterring monopolistic behavior. The commission was hindered in fulfilling its objectives by court decisions that circumscribed its law enforcement efforts, vocal opposition from many members of Congress, and a lack of cooperation from businesses. For much of the 1920s, the nation prospered during the administrations of Republican presidents Warren Harding and Calvin Coolidge. At the same time, the FTC, under the direction of conservative, probusiness chairmen, embraced a more trusting and cooperative attitude toward business and cut back on its regulatory programs.

During the Great Depression, the severe economic decline that began with the 1929 stock market crash and lasted for more than a decade, the FTC fell into decline because the federal government, under the National Industrial Recovery Act (NIRA), wrote the rules on fair competition. Any attempt by the FTC to enforce antitrust laws would have conflicted with the government's efforts to revitalize the nation's struggling economy. However, beginning in 1936, Congress passed several acts that enhanced the commission's legal authority, including the Robinson-Patman Act of 1936 (which made it easier for the FTC to police unfair price concessions given by manufacturers to large buyers), the Wool Products Labeling Act of 1939 (which authorized the FTC to draft and enforce substantive rules governing practices in that specific industry), and the Wheeler-Lea Act (which prohibited deceptive and unfair practices in commerce). Congress increased the commission's appropriations to enable it to meet its new responsibilities, and the FTC's initial efforts in the area of consumer protection, particularly its efforts to prohibit deceptive advertising practices, were well received. After the Supreme Court declared the NIRA unconstitutional, the FTC revived its antitrust enforcement efforts.

Following World War II, the FTC continued its involvement in consumer protection but began to scale down its prosecutorial approach to antitrust cases. During the 1950s and 1960s, the FTC attempted to prevent unfair methods of competition by establishing guidelines for business practices and encouraging voluntary cooperation by the business community. The chairmen during this period also sought to establish a more cooperative relationship between the commission and the business community.

In the late 1960s, a number of critics and reports by special committees had leveled charges that the FTC had fallen short of its statutory objectives. The Nader Report on the Federal Trade Commission ridiculed the FTC's pursuit of trivial cases and called for Chairman Paul Rand Dixon's resignation. The commission, said the report, suffered from political cronyism, had become bogged down in bureaucratic red tape, and had often failed to take the initiative in consumer fraud cases. These criticisms, which were echoed by a special study group commissioned by the American Bar Association (ABA), finally led to a reorganization and revitalization of the FTC during the early 1970s.

When Congress enacted the Magnuson-Moss Act in 1975, it dramatically strengthened the authority of the FTC. The act empowered the FTC to establish industrywide trade regulations that would set standards of acceptable business practices. However, by the end of the decade, conservative critics charged that the commission had gone overboard in its consumer protection program. The FTC's aggressive consumer protection efforts, particularly those directed at regulating children's advertising, led the *Washington Post* to label the FTC the National Nanny.

When President Ronald Reagan took office in 1981, the FTC was one target of his plan to reduce the size and scope of the federal regulatory agencies. The FTC's budget and staff steadily shrank during the Reagan administration, and the commission pursued fewer consumer protection and antitrust cases. In 1989, the ABA published a study that sharply criticized the reduction in the FTC's staff and resources and questioned whether the commission was fulfilling its legislative objectives. Despite the problems that the government now faces in reducing the federal budget deficit, FTC chairman Janet D. Steiger has promised to try once again to make the FTC an effective guardian of the marketplace.

Today the FTC's staff of about 920 people deals with issues that affect the lives of most Americans. The care and content labels that are sewn in clothes, the energy consumption information that comes with a new appliance, the

In December 1990, Denis Breen (left), an assistant director for antitrust in the Bureau of Economics, and staff economists Tim Deyak (center) and Margaret Patterson (right) discuss an ongoing antitrust law-enforcement investigation. FTC staffers attempt to preserve a free marketplace for the benefit of consumers and honest businesses.

octane ratings on gasoline pumps, and the warranty disclosure stickers that are posted on used cars for sale by dealers are the result of the consumer protection programs of the FTC. Through the development of regulations and guidelines, the review of proposed mergers, and case-by-case law enforcement, the FTC works to preserve a free marketplace in which competition protects the livelihood of honest businesses and affords consumers a vast array of goods and services at the lowest possible prices.

In 1885, a railroad construction crew pauses on an overpass in the Cascade Range. As the Industrial Revolution took hold in the United States in the 19th century, advances in transportation (such as transcontinental railroads), communication, and manufacturing led to the rise of highly concentrated businesses. Concern over the abuses of big business led to calls for a federal agency to regulate business, resulting in the creation of the FTC in 1914.

TWO

The Business of the
United States Is
Business

On March 9, 1776, a little less than a year after the firing of the "shot heard round the world" that started the American Revolution, *The Wealth of Nations*, a book written by economist Adam Smith, was published in London. *The Wealth of Nations* provided the philosophical underpinnings of the economic system now called the free-enterprise system, or capitalism. Smith believed that human behavior can be fundamentally explained by the rational and persistent pursuit of economic self-interest. As a result of individuals striving to increase their own wealth, reasoned Smith, society in general would also benefit. Self-interest is the "invisible hand" that drives the marketplace and a competitive private enterprise economy. Nothing could be worse than government altering the course of the natural economy by enacting reformist legislation and establishing bureaucratic regulation.

U.S. businessmen shared Smith's view that self-interest and the "invisible hand" of the market resulted in the public good. The new nation presented many opportunities for entrepreneurs. With local communities separated from each other by poor transportation and poor communication facilities, small enterprises concentrated on local markets. Although individual efforts contributed to the rapid building of a great nation, the United States—with a vast continent to tame and abundant supplies of natural resources—evolved in the direction of industrialization and specialization. Eli Whitney's cotton gin, invented in 1793, enabled cotton production in the South to account for a significant portion of the U.S. economy. Oceangoing vessels continued to expand trade beyond the nation's borders.

There were dramatic developments in transportation and communication. The invention of the steamboat by Robert Fulton in 1811 made commerce on inland waterways a reality. However, some states granted monopolies to select steamboat owners, which inhibited the carriage of people and goods. In *Gibbons v. Ogden* (1824), the Supreme Court struck down a New York law that granted a partnership the exclusive right to engage in steamboat navigation in the waters of New York. The decision upheld the supremacy of the federal government in interstate commerce and outlawed steamboat monopolies. By 1830, nearly 200 steamboats were operating on the nation's western rivers.

During the first half of the 19th century, railroads also passed from the experimental stage into an extensive operational system, and by 1861 telegraph lines spanned the continent. The Civil War not only created

Robert Fulton's steamboat Clermont *maneuvers up the Hudson River during a trial run in 1811. In 1824, the Supreme Court outlawed monopolies granted by states to certain steamboat operators. The monopolies hampered interstate commerce by inhibiting the carriage of people and goods on the nation's waterways.*

unprecedented demand for the transportation of armies and the production of munitions, it spurred a trend toward concentration of workers and machines in one place to manufacture products of uniform size and characteristics.

The movement toward industrial concentration also stimulated the development of a new form of doing business. Sole proprietorships and small partnerships were not equal to the task of managing large amounts of capital or economic power. Only the corporation offered the benefits of limited liability, free transfer of ownership interests, and perpetual existence not tied to any one individual. After 1850, the states began passing general incorporation statutes, which provided an easy way to form a corporation in comparison to the old practice of incorporating businesses by special acts of Congress or state legislatures.

Armed with the ability to incorporate their enterprises, entrepreneurs began to search for efficiency and market power. At that time, each transfer of a product from one company to another was subject to a six percent federal tax. It became advantageous to integrate the stages of manufacturing—from the supplier of raw materials to the fabricator and finisher to the distributor—into one enterprise. Such vertical integration also allowed the sources of supply and distribution to be controlled so that competitors could not easily enter the market.

The concentration of business began with the railroads. Entrepreneurs such as Cornelius Vanderbilt and Jay Gould tried to control long stretches of track so that they could set the rates. Businesses in industries dependent on the railroads tried to secure special rate reductions. John D. Rockefeller's Standard Oil Company of Ohio had such significant market power in Cleveland that it was able to negotiate secret rebates from the railroads, enabling the company to undersell its competitors. Sometimes Standard Oil sold its products at prices below cost in selected markets and then charged higher prices after the competition had been driven out of the market. By 1872, Rockefeller had eliminated competition in Cleveland and controlled about 20 percent of the refining facilities in the nation. He triumphantly declared that the movement toward monopoly was "the origin of the whole system of modern economic administration. . . . The day of combination is here to stay. Individualism has gone, never to return."

The ideas of the era, including the concept of "social Darwinism," based on the theory of evolution announced by Charles Darwin in *The Origin of Species* (1859), seemed to support the rise of industrial tycoons. The growth of a large business, said Rockefeller, "is merely a survival of the fittest." Through their corporations, the robber barons, as they became known, entered into trust

A cartoon lampoons the eminence of oil magnate John D. Rockefeller, who began building his industrial empire in the 1860s. Through his company, Standard Oil, Rockefeller amassed a personal fortune of more than $1 billion. In 1911, however, the Supreme Court declared that Standard Oil was a monopoly in restraint of trade and thereby illegal under the Sherman Antitrust Act.

agreements through which they divided up markets or combined to control the production and the prices of certain commodities. While accumulating vast fortunes, the robber barons also oversaw the building of big cities, the rapid development of industrialism, and the concentration of power, wealth, and prestige in a few industrial giants.

The trustification of the United States contributed to higher prices and higher costs of living for consumers. The farmers and others who formed the Grange movement in the late 1860s first promoted the idea that government should regulate the monopolistic corporations. Later, during the first administration of Grover Cleveland, a committee led by Senator Shelby Cullom of Illinois investigated the railroads and concluded that "upon no public question are the people nearly so unanimous" than that Congress should regulate interstate commerce. The Interstate Commerce Act of 1887 created the first independent regulatory agency. However, the Interstate Commerce Commission initially proved to be ineffective because the railroads soon evaded its regulations.

The public's desire to curb the monopolistic tendencies of big business was so deep that when the Sherman Antitrust Act came up for a vote in the summer of 1890, it passed both houses of Congress with only one dissenting vote. The Sherman Act prohibited agreements among firms to fix prices or other terms of trade and efforts to monopolize trade or commerce. But even the most ardent proponents of the Sherman Act agreed that, at least as enforced and interpreted by the courts in the late 19th century, it did not control the trusts. The act was used infrequently because once monopolistic behavior reached the level of a violation of the Sherman Act, the damage had been done and the resulting anticompetitive combination was difficult to unravel. If anything, the pace of corporate combinations seemed to increase.

The federal government began to make the first serious effort to enforce the Sherman Act during the administration of President Theodore Roosevelt. Roosevelt, the popularly proclaimed "trust buster," was fond of ridiculing the "malefactors of great wealth." During the first weeks after Roosevelt took office in September 1901, following the assassination of President William McKinley, one of the most conspicuous of these malefactors, steel magnate J. Pierpont Morgan, combined the stock of the Union Pacific, Northern Pacific, and Burlington railroads into the Northern Securities Company.

Roosevelt instructed Attorney General Philander Knox to file a lawsuit against Morgan and Northern Securities alleging that they had illegally conspired to restrain trade. The Supreme Court ruled in 1904 that the Northern Securities merger violated the Sherman Act because the mere

An 1873 poster provides an idealized view of the farm organization popularly known as the National Grange. The Grange was the first group to advocate that the federal government should regulate monopolies.

existence of a combination in restraint of trade, no matter how reasonable, was a per se (automatic) violation of the law. The dissolution of Northern Securities proved, at last, that the federal government was more powerful than J. P. Morgan.

The Supreme Court's ruling in the Northern Securities case, however, did not stop the trend toward consolidation. In 1911, John D. Rockefeller, who headed the only other great financial empire that could rival Morgan's, faced the Supreme Court. In *Standard Oil Company of New Jersey v. U.S.*, the Court ruled that the Sherman Act did not prohibit all restraints of trade, contracts, or conspiracies, but only unreasonable ones. This "rule of reason" has been applied in analyzing combinations in restraint of trade ever since.

As the courts relaxed the rigid lines drawn by the Sherman Act, the argument for greater government regulation of business gathered strength. During the presidential election of 1912, the idea of a federal agency to regulate business became a campaign issue. The Republican platform, on which President William Howard Taft ran for reelection, proposed a commission to "promote promptness in the administration of the [antitrust] law and avoid delays and technicalities incidental to court procedure." Former President Theodore Roosevelt and his "Bull Moose" followers (so named because Roosevelt had declared himself as "fit as a Bull Moose") formed the Progressive party, which advocated a "strong National regulation of inter-State corporations" and promised to establish a "strong Federal administrative commission" that would use publicity, supervision, and regulation to control monopolistic power.

Woodrow Wilson, the Democratic candidate, said his party was against private monopoly and for the vigorous enforcement of the civil and criminal antitrust laws. Wilson, the governor of New Jersey and former president of Princeton University, was influenced by Louis D. Brandeis, a leading progressive lawyer whom he met a few months before the election. Brandeis, who later became a Supreme Court justice, was an outspoken proponent of regulated competition and economic freedom for small businesses.

Wilson won the election, but although he had campaigned on a platform of restoring free competition, his administration granted organized labor an exemption from the antitrust laws in June 1913 and waited until November of that year before consulting with Democratic congressional leaders on how best to proceed with the administration's economic agenda. Most Democrats wanted a new statute that would better define restraints of trade, prohibit interlocking directorates (the practice of sharing directors among different corporations), and clarify the "rule of reason" announced by the Supreme Court in 1911. A minority of Democrats and most progressive Republicans thought that it would be impossible to define every restraint of trade in a statute and that what was needed was an independent trade commission with authority to outlaw unfair competition.

27

In a cartoon from the early 1900s, President Theodore Roosevelt confronts the influential industrialists and financiers of the era—Jay Gould, James J. Hill, J. P. Morgan, John D. Rockefeller, and the Oxnard brothers—on Wall Street. Roosevelt initiated the federal government's first serious efforts to enforce the Sherman Antitrust Act, which prohibited anticompetitive practices and efforts to monopolize trade or commerce.

Louis D. Brandeis, a lawyer who was an outspoken proponent of regulated competition, free enterprise, and economic freedom for small businesses, helped draft the Federal Trade Commission Act of 1914. The act established the FTC and authorized it to investigate, publicize, and prohibit all unfair methods of competition.

Meanwhile, the U.S. Chamber of Commerce promoted a statute that would prohibit unfair trade practices and establish a friendly trade commission to give advice to businesses and to determine what practices were legal and illegal.

Brandeis advocated a strong trade commission and persuaded Wilson, who was suspicious of the special interests represented by big bankers, big manufacturers, and "big masters of commerce," to take up the cause. Brandeis and his close friend George L. Rublee drafted a bill that outlawed (but did not define) unfair trade practices and established a trade commission with broad authority to oversee business activity and to issue cease and desist orders to prevent unfair methods of competition. The trade commission's authority to prohibit unfair methods of competition would allow it to stop practices before they could mature into full-fledged violations of the Sherman Antitrust Act. Congress accepted the Brandeis-Rublee bill and enacted it under its official name, the Federal Trade Commission Act. Wilson signed the act into law on September 10, 1914.

That same year, Representative Henry Clayton, chairman of the House Judiciary Committee, drafted the original versions of three bills that would become known as the Clayton Act. Both the FTC and the Department of

Joseph E. Davies, the former commissioner of corporations in the Department of Commerce's Bureau of Corporations, was the first chairman of the FTC. He headed the commission from 1915 to 1918.

Justice are empowered to enforce this act. It prohibits specific types of anticompetitive conduct with respect to "commodities" and allows private individuals who have been injured by anticompetitive conduct forbidden in the antitrust laws to sue for three times the amount of damages that they have incurred. The act outlaws the purchase by a corporation of stock of another corporation if the effect of such an acquisition would be to restrain commerce or create a monopoly. It also prohibits so-called tying contracts that require buyers to deal exclusively with certain sellers and prohibits certain interlocking directorates among corporations and banks over a certain size.

When the new FTC commissioners were sworn into office on March 16, 1915, they selected Joseph E. Davies, who had been commissioner of corporations in the Department of Commerce's Bureau of Corporations, as the first chairman. The Bureau of Corporations had broad powers to investigate the kinds of practices that had generated the desire for a federal trade commission, but it had no enforcement powers and simply issued reports. The

30

FTC staff consisted largely of holdovers from the Bureau of Corporations, and the commission moved into the bureau's old offices in the Commerce Department building. Despite its space problems (hearings were held in the chairman's office), the FTC went right to work. The commission's first three complaints involved the false labeling and advertising of cotton as silk. In all, the FTC issued 40 complaints and held 114 conferences with industry leaders in its first 4 months. George Rublee, an architect of the FTC Act and one of the first FTC commissioners, wrote the original rules of FTC practice and established a case-by-case approach to identify unfair methods of competition. The commission also established the practice of investigating each case before issuing a formal complaint.

While the nation was fighting in World War I, the FTC, at Wilson's request, conducted a controversial study of the meat-packing industry. Just as the publication of Upton Sinclair's novel about industrial greed and workers' misery in the meat-packing industry, *The Jungle* (1906), had earlier outraged the public, the FTC's study of the industry provoked such an uproar in Congress that some members called for an investigation of the FTC and its purportedly socialist employees. The U.S. Chamber of Commerce denounced the FTC in a 1918 issue of *Nation's Business* for using "broad accusation and innuendo" and issuing biased and inaccurate publicity releases. As a result, Congress, under the Packers and Stockyards Act of 1921, gave the job of regulating the meat packers and stockyards to the secretary of agriculture rather than the FTC and eliminated funds for future FTC investigations of the industry.

In 1919, in the first court test of the FTC Act, the U.S. Court of Appeals for the Seventh Circuit upheld the FTC's cease and desist order against Sears Roebuck & Company, which had published an advertisement that falsely claimed that its sugar and tea were cheaper because Sears was such a large company and could buy goods in bulk. The court ruled that the FTC had jurisdiction over deceptive practices regardless of whether they had a direct effect on competition. After the victory in the *Sears* case, however, the courts joined Congress in curtailing the power of the reform-minded FTC. In *FTC v. Gratz* (1920), the first FTC case to reach the Supreme Court, the Court ruled, "The words 'unfair methods of competition' are not defined by the statute, and their exact meaning is in dispute. It is for the courts, not the Commission, ultimately to determine what they include." As a result of *Gratz*, the FTC could not proceed against anticompetitive practices unless they had been held to be fraudulent, predatory, or otherwise deceptive by the courts prior to 1914 or clearly violated the Sherman Act.

That same year, although U.S. Steel owned 85 percent of the nation's steel manufacturing capacity, the Supreme Court ruled in *U.S. v. United States Steel* (1920) that the company had not restrained trade or attempted to monopolize the industry in violation of the Sherman Act. Corporate size, by itself, did not constitute a violation of the law. Finally, in *FTC v. Curtis Publishing Company* (1923), the Supreme Court held that the courts, not the FTC, were to decide whether leases, sales agreements, or understandings substantially lessened competition or tended to create a monopoly. In *The Federal Trade Commission* (1924), the first major study of the FTC, Gerard C. Henderson characterized the FTC as "little more than a subordinate adjunct to the judicial system" that had achieved "meager results."

By the early 1920s, the mood of the country clearly was changing. President Warren G. Harding proclaimed, "What we want in America is less government in business and more business in government." As a result of being stymied by the judiciary and intimidated by Congress, the FTC began to retreat into a program of largely voluntary and cooperative regulation.

Harding's death in August 1923 brought Calvin Coolidge to the White House. Coolidge ensured an ideological change at the FTC when he appointed former Washington congressman William E. Humphrey as the new chairman in 1925. Humphrey, who felt that the commission had become "an instrument of oppression and disturbance instead of a help to business," promptly announced that the FTC would no longer serve as a "publicity bureau to spread socialistic propaganda." Under Humphrey and the commission's first Republican majority, settlements were negotiated in secret and retained in confidential files to protect businesses from harmful publicity.

In accordance with Coolidge's declaration that "the business of the United States is business," the FTC cut back its regulation of commerce, stepped up its efforts to provide advice and assistance, prepared studies requested by Congress, and held trade-practice conferences. The Supreme Court erased any doubts about the commission's new direction in *FTC v. American Tobacco* (1924), in which the Court precluded the FTC from involving itself in "fishing expeditions into private papers on the possibility that they may disclose evidence of a crime."

Under Humphrey, the hostility between the FTC and business came to an end. The 1927 *Magazine of Wall Street* reported that Humphrey had changed the FTC from a "hectoring, tyrannical and . . . tireless snooper" into an "instrument of protection." No longer was the commission to be the "crusading, muck-raking body" that the *Wall Street Journal* dubbed it in 1925.

William E. Humphrey, a vocal opponent of the FTC, became the commission's chairman in 1925. During Humphrey's nine-year tenure, the FTC scaled down its regulation of commerce and sought to encourage industrial self-regulation.

Buoyed by the tax-cutting policies of Secretary of the Treasury Andrew Mellon and the encouragement of cooperation among businessmen by Secretary of Commerce Herbert Hoover, a new wave of corporate consolidation swept the nation during the 1920s. The mergers spurred speculation in dubious investments, which helped fuel the great stock market crash of October 1929 that occurred seven months after Hoover became president.

During the Great Depression and the New Deal, the FTC went into full retreat. President Franklin D. Roosevelt embarked on a drastic program to revitalize the nation's paralyzed economy and to restore confidence in the securities markets so that capital could be raised for U.S. industry. He recruited James M. Landis, head of the FTC's securities division, to help draft new securities legislation. Although the responsibility for enforcing the Securities Act of 1933 rested initially with the FTC, it was turned over the following year to the new Securities and Exchange Commission (SEC). *92-18482*

Regulation and enforcement of the antitrust laws were not high on Roosevelt's agenda. Under the National Industrial Recovery Act (NIRA), which established the National Recovery Administration, business practices were governed by 746 Codes of Fair Competition that set minimum prices and standards for products and business practices. So long as they adhered to these codes, businesses had no reason to fear prosecution under the antitrust laws. After the Supreme Court ruled that the NIRA was unconstitutional as an improper delegation of legislative power to the executive branch in *Schechter Poultry Corporation v. United States* (1935), the FTC dismissed the complaints that it had filed under the Codes of Fair Competition.

During the mid-1930s, Senator Joseph Robinson and Representative Wright Patman collaborated to draft legislation prohibiting certain anticompetitive business practices exposed in a series of FTC reports on price discrimination by chain stores. The FTC reports alleged that chain stores were able to negotiate price discounts and other favorable terms of trade from wholesalers that were unavailable to smaller mom-and-pop stores. Congressional hearings suggested that the Great Atlantic & Pacific Tea Company had received discriminatory price breaks and allowances totaling $8 million in 1 year without passing along comparable price breaks to consumers. The Robinson-Patman Act of 1936 amended the Clayton Act to make it easier to prevent discrimination in prices, allowances, commissions, or services. A number of defenses are built into the Robinson-Patman Act. For example, reducing prices to meet lower prices offered by other firms is permissible. Ironically, although the act was supposed to protect small businesses, it has been more frequently enforced against smaller companies than large corporations.

A chain of court defeats in the 1930s also prompted Congress to expand the FTC's authority. In *FTC v. Raladam* (1931), the Supreme Court held that the FTC could not issue an order to stop false advertising in the absence of proof that the advertisement injured competitors even if it deceived consumers. In 1938, the Wheeler-Lea Act amended Section 5 of the FTC Act to prohibit unfair or deceptive acts and practices in commerce, as well as unfair methods of competition. This allowed the FTC to protect consumers as well as businesses from dishonest trade practices. It also meant that the FTC no longer had to prove that an unfair or deceptive practice had an anticompetitive effect before taking action. The Wheeler-Lea amendments also enhanced the FTC's authority to prohibit false advertising of food, drugs, cosmetics, and consumer goods. In addition, the FTC was authorized to seek civil penalties (fines) in federal court in the event of violations of its cease and desist orders. The Wool Products Labeling Act of 1939 allowed the FTC for the first time to develop rules regulating business practices in a particular industry.

In 1942, Ethel Oxley stands in her drugstore in Southington, Connecticut. As a result of a series of FTC reports in the mid-1930s, Congress passed the Robinson-Patman Act of 1936 to outlaw discrimination in prices, allowances, commissions, and services that gave large chain stores a competitive edge over small mom-and-pop businesses such as Oxley's.

During the 1940s, the FTC's economists devoted themselves to establishing the facts to support amendments to remedy the weaknesses of the Clayton Act. After the Supreme Court ruled that the FTC could not order a divestiture because it had not issued the divestiture order before a company had acquired a competitor's assets, the FTC stopped issuing cease and desist orders under the Clayton Act. Instead, the FTC issued a series of reports concerning the possible extinction of small firms as a result of mergers of different and sometimes completely unrelated business activities into conglomerates.

The FTC also had trouble keeping its own house in order. To remedy that situation, a Planning Council was established at the FTC in October 1947 to identify problem areas and recommend appropriate allocation of the commission's resources. Once again the critics of the FTC gained the upper hand. The 1949 assessment of the FTC by the Hoover Committee Task Force's Report on Regulatory Commissions concluded:

> As the years have progressed, the Commission has become immersed in a multitude of petty problems; it has not probed into new areas of anticompetitive practices; it has become increasingly bogged down with cumbersome procedures and inordinate delays in disposition of cases. Its economic work—instead of being the backbone of the Commission—has been allowed to dwindle almost to none. The Commission has largely become a passive judicial agency, waiting for cases to come up on the docket, under routinized procedures, without active responsibility for achieving statutory objectives.

Congressman Estes Kefauver of Tennessee had already reached the same conclusion. In a congressional report, he noted that between 1932 and 1947, the FTC had brought antitrust actions covering only one-third of the 121 products in industries in which the top 4 producers accounted for more than 75 percent of production. Of the 107 largest manufacturers, the Monopoly Subcommittee Report identified only 15 that had been the subject of an FTC case. Kefauver teamed up with Representative Emanuel Celler of New York to propose the Celler-Kefauver Antimerger Act of 1950. The act amended Section 7 of the Clayton Act to remedy the omission that had plagued the FTC's antimerger program since 1926—the commission's lack of authority to prevent or undo mergers that were accomplished by means of asset acquisitions rather than purchases of company stock. Since Section 7 of the Clayton Act prohibited incipient (developing) violations of the Sherman Act—that is,

In October 1973, Lee K. Thorpe, owner of Thorpe Furs in Evanston, Illinois, examines a new shipment of furs from Greece. The FTC has the authority to administer and enforce the Fur Products Labeling Act, which requires the labeling of fur articles in wearing apparel (which should include the name of the animal from which the fur was taken and whether it is dyed) and the truthful invoicing and advertising of furs and fur products.

acquisitions that might lessen competition or tend to create a monopoly—it became one of the favorite weapons in the antitrust war.

During the 1950s, Congress gave the FTC additional authority under the Fur Products Labeling Act, the Flammable Fabrics Act, and the Textile Fiber Products Identification Act. In general, these laws required labels, advertising, and invoicing for products to be truthful and to disclose the amount of genuine fur or fiber contained in the product.

The panels on the doors of the FTC building illustrate the progress of shipping in the United States: from Columbus's fleet (top row, left) to a large seaplane (bottom row, right). The door panels on three other entrances represent the nation's development in foreign trade, agriculture, and industry.

THREE

Changing with the Times

Upon assuming the presidency in 1953, Dwight D. Eisenhower promised a new Republican era and a new FTC. The commission's new chairman, Edward Howrey, instituted a purge that resulted in the departure of several Democratic staff members who had previously opposed Howrey when he appeared before the commission as a lawyer defending large corporations. The FTC also lost the three top economists who had authored a study of the efforts of major oil companies to restrain trade.

Howrey quickly instituted a new theory of antitrust based more explicitly on economic analysis. Before the FTC would act, he wanted evidence of actual anticompetitive effects, rather than evidence of market shares, to establish restraints of trade. As a practical matter, *Business Week* observed, an FTC lawyer would be hard-pressed to find enough evidence to satisfy the criteria for antitrust enforcement that Howrey had instituted. After only two years in office, Howrey resigned amid allegations of influence peddling and conflicts of interest. But he continued to exert influence over the FTC from the law firm he subsequently joined. Howrey left behind many staffers whom he had appointed to the FTC, including his handpicked successor, John Gwynne, a former conservative Republican congressman.

When Gwynne left in May 1959, he was succeeded by former FTC general counsel Earl Kintner. Kintner was supportive of the staff and the agency's law enforcement mission. He favored assisting industry to obey the law by establishing guidelines for business practices. He also organized the first consumer conference sponsored by the FTC. Kintner fostered an aggressive approach to trial work and made the agency a good place for young lawyers to work. When Democrat John F. Kennedy assumed the presidency in 1961, Kintner left to become a senior partner at a Washington law firm. Before entering office, Kennedy asked James Landis, former FTC commissioner and former chairman of the SEC, to study the federal regulatory agencies. Landis's report recommended that there be a "czar" in the White House to oversee the agencies. Kennedy concluded that this was not politically feasible, but the Landis report spawned reorganization plans for a number of agencies, including the FTC.

Kennedy appointed Paul Rand Dixon as the new chairman. Dixon, who had been with the FTC from 1938 to 1957, abandoned the FTC's policy of emphasizing case-by-case enforcement and sought instead to implement broad regulatory policies. Although the number of FTC employees increased from about 700 to 1,150, cases placed on the litigation docket declined from 503 to 49. Litigation was effectively stalled, and voluntary compliance was emphasized.

During the Dixon era, the FTC did achieve several major consumer protection victories. On January 11, 1964, the surgeon general of the Public Health Service issued a report counseling, "Cigarette smoking is a health hazard of sufficient importance . . . to warrant appropriate remedial action." Based on this report, the FTC issued a notice of a proposed rule that would require cigarette advertising and labeling to contain a warning of the product's health hazard. The rule, as finally adopted in June 1964, stated that "it is an unfair or deceptive act or practice . . . to fail to disclose, clearly and prominently, in all advertising and on every pack or other container . . . that cigarette smoking is dangerous to health and may cause death from cancer and other diseases."

Opposition, particularly from the tobacco states, led the House Interstate and Foreign Commerce Committee to request the FTC to postpone the effective date of its rule from January to July 1965. The FTC agreed, but in its next session, Congress enacted a law that superseded the commission's rule. As the House report stated: "The Committee feels that at the present time the necessity for, and the effectiveness of this requirement has not been demon-

In 1988, workers put the finishing touches on a billboard that advertises a brand of cigarettes. In 1964, the FTC announced that it would issue a rule requiring cigarette advertising and labeling to include the surgeon general's warning about the health hazards connected with smoking. Under pressure from tobacco manufacturers, Congress intervened and enacted a law that required a less forceful warning.

strated." The new law required that packages contain the statement "Caution: Cigarette smoking may be hazardous to your health."

Several other legislative milestones during the Dixon era gave the FTC new responsibilities. The Flammable Fabrics Act Amendments of 1967 sought to prevent the needless burning of children wearing non-flame-resistant sleepwear. The 1968 Truth-in-Lending Law required that the cost of credit be disclosed in a uniform way. Finally, the Fair Packaging and Labeling Act required that all packages identify their contents, the name and place of business of the manufacturer or distributor, and the net weight of the package contents.

During the summer of 1968, seven youthful volunteers roamed the halls of the FTC seeking information for a special report. The resulting Nader Report on the Federal Trade Commission, issued in January 1969, focused on consumer protection and promptly created a scandal. It depicted an agency controlled by cronyism, mired in trivia, and unwilling and unable to do its job. The ABA, at the request of President Richard Nixon, appointed a commission headed by Miles W. Kirkpatrick to study the FTC and make recommendations for its future activities and its organization. The ABA's report, issued on September 15, 1969, just a few weeks before a scheduled vacancy on the commission, led to the end of Dixon's term as chairman. The ABA report criticized the FTC for failing to set goals and priorities, for mismanaging staff and resources, for pursuing trivial matters, and for curtailing its enforcement efforts. "The case for change is plain," it said. Hearings were held on Capitol Hill, and the FTC's congressional overseers asked the commission to propose remedies for the deficiencies identified in the reports.

Nixon appointed Caspar Weinberger, former finance director of California, as the new FTC chairman and called for a "reactivation and revitalization of the FTC." Within six months after he was named as FTC chairman, Weinberger became the head of the revamped Office of Management and Budget (OMB). During his brief tenure, Weinberger did manage to reorganize the FTC along functional antitrust and consumer protection lines by establishing the Bureau of Competition and the Bureau of Consumer Protection. He abolished other bureaus, closed hundreds of marginal investigations, and discharged more than half of the top-level staff.

The revitalization of the FTC continued under the next chairman, Miles W. Kirkpatrick. Kirkpatrick, who had chaired the ABA's committee that studied the FTC, deftly picked up where Weinberger left off and began the process of weeding out the dead wood in the commission's professional staff. Less productive attorneys were offered the option of resigning or being fired. Others were transferred from Washington to the Kansas City regional office (which was abolished in the mid-1970s). In all, nearly a third of the middle- and lower-level staff was replaced. At the same time, Kirkpatrick initiated an effort to hire highly talented young lawyers committed to aggressive law enforcement.

Under Kirkpatrick's leadership, the FTC issued a complaint against the four largest producers of ready-to-eat breakfast cereals, in *Kellogg Co. et al.* The complaint charged them with violating the FTC Act by maintaining a highly concentrated, noncompetitive market structure and by obtaining, sharing, and exercising monopoly power in that market. This innovative concept of a "shared monopoly" among the handful of companies that controlled almost all of the business was the brainchild of Charles Mueller, an FTC lawyer who read and appreciated economics. The *Kellogg* case resulted in a fierce battle between the FTC and the industry, with Congress participating from the sidelines as critic and observer. Ultimately, in the early 1980s the FTC dismissed the complaint because there was not enough evidence to prove its allegations.

Kirkpatrick's tenure also included the Supreme Court's landmark decision in *FTC v. Sperry & Hutchinson* (1972), in which the Court confirmed that the FTC could define and proscribe a practice because it was unfair even if it was not deceptive and did not offend the letter or spirit of the antitrust laws. Kirkpatrick resigned in February 1973 to return to law practice after authorizing the FTC's landmark opinion in the *Pfizer* case that required the company to have evidence of facts to substantiate an advertising claim. Kirkpatrick's departure capped the period from 1967 to 1973 when Congress enacted more than 25 separate federal regulatory laws, including the National Environmental Policy Act, the Consumer Product Safety Act, the Clean Air Act Amendments, and the Truth-in-Lending Act.

Kirkpatrick was succeeded by Lewis Engman, a Harvard-trained lawyer, who served from 1973 to 1975. At hearings preceding Engman's swearing in as chairman, Senator Ted Stevens told Engman, "I am really hopeful . . . that you will become a real zealot in terms of consumer affairs and some of these big business people will complain to us that you are going too far." Soon thereafter, Stevens got his wish when the FTC instituted a requirement that major corporations report financial data by line of business and when the FTC filed a complaint against several petroleum industry firms in a case known as *In re Exxon* (1973). This case reflected a shift in the direction of antitrust enforcement at the FTC toward attempts to break up concentrated industries in which a few firms controlled a large share of the market. Like the *Kellogg* case, the *Exxon* case was dismissed in 1981, the first year of the Reagan presidency. Concerns about the problems the FTC encountered in its petroleum investigation led to the enactment in November 1973 of the Alaska Pipeline Act. A number of provisions in the act give FTC attorneys new authority to go to court and to obtain temporary and, in some cases, permanent

A facsimile of an S & H Green Stamp. In the early 1970s, the FTC charged Sperry and Hutchinson, a trading stamp company, with using unfair trade practices in its efforts to control the redemption of its stamps. In FTC v. Sperry & Hutchinson *(1972), the Supreme Court held that the FTC could define a practice as unfair even if it was not deceptive.*

injunctions if they believe that a violation of a law enforced by the FTC has occurred or is about to occur. This injunction authority has proved to be a potent weapon for the FTC.

Sometimes Engman used informal methods to evaluate how proposed policies might work in the real world. When the FTC staff recommended that nutrition information be included in 30- and 60-second television ads, he asked for an example of how this might be accomplished. The commissioners viewed a staff-produced sample advertisement that contained nutrition information. When Engman asked each one what they remembered, the commissioners each said there had been some "stuff" there. The nutrition-information advertising proposal was killed.

Although the FTC had long argued that the FTC Act granted it the authority to issue rules, the commission did not issue any substantive trade regulations prior to 1962. Between 1962 and 1970, in addition to the proposed cigarette-labeling rule, some cautious and narrowly drawn interpretive rules appeared. Then the commission issued the Octane Posting Rule in 1971, which compelled gasoline retailers to post the octane ratings of their gasoline on the pumps. It also issued the cooling-off provisions of the Door-to-Door Sales Rule in 1972, which required that companies that market products by visiting consumers at home give consumers three days within which to change their mind and cancel the purchase. These rules undertook to remedy as well as define deception. The Octane Rule was challenged by the petroleum industry, but the U.S. Court of Appeals for the District of Columbia Circuit upheld the rule in *National Petroleum Refiners Association v. FTC* (1973), concluding that the FTC had the authority to promulgate substantive trade regulation rules.

The FTC's authority to promulgate trade regulation rules to prevent unfair or deceptive acts or practices was confirmed by the passage in 1975 of the Magnuson-Moss Warranty–FTC Improvement Act. Described by Miles Kirk-patrick (then a lawyer in private practice) as "the legal equivalent of dynamite and a veritable unsprung bear trap," the FTC Improvement Act provided for industrywide rule-making proceedings that would result in substantive rules that would apply to an entire industry with the force of law. It also established significant civil penalties of up to $10,000 for each knowing violation of a trade regulation rule. Perhaps most significantly, it effectively remedied a setback delivered by the U.S. Court of Appeals for the Ninth Circuit, which ruled in *Heater v. FTC* (1974) that the commission could not itself grant consumer redress. The FTC Improvement Act authorized the FTC to go to federal court to obtain consumer redress, such as the voiding of contracts, refunds, the return of property, money damages, and public notification of the violation, after the FTC had issued an order against the firm's illegal practices.

In 1975, the FTC initiated proposed rule-making proceedings covering over-the-counter drugs advertising, food advertising, unfair credit practices, mobile-home sales and service, and hearing aids. Later, funeral industry practices, health spas, and used cars became the subjects of proposed trade regulation rules. The revitalization begun in the early 1970s was in full flower.

When Engman resigned in 1975, President Gerald Ford appointed Calvin Collier, formerly the FTC's general counsel, as the new chairman. Collier continued the improvement of management initiated by Engman and presided over the maturation of rule-making proceedings initiated under the Magnuson-Moss Act. He also was chairman at the time of the enactment of the Hart-Scott-Rodino Antitrust Improvements Act of 1976 (HSR Act), which required businesses to notify the FTC and the Justice Department's Antitrust Division of a planned merger before it takes place and to delay the merger for a certain period of time while the FTC and the Justice Department decide whether to challenge the merger.

After taking office, President Jimmy Carter appointed Michael Pertschuk, staff director of the Senate Commerce Committee, as FTC chairman. Under the four chairmen who preceded Pertschuk, the FTC staff had grown in quality and vitality as well as in numbers. Its lawyers came from more prestigious law schools, and its targets were no longer the trivial but firms with broad influence upon the economy and consumers.

Pertschuk viewed himself as one of the "Scarlet Pimpernels" of the consumer movement: those who were secret, or at least unsung, heroes doing good by exposing and preventing corporate abuse. Planting himself firmly on the side of the angels, Pertschuk appointed consumer activists to significant FTC positions. By 1978, many of the 15 industrywide trade regulation rules initiated in the mid-1970s were nearing the end of the rule-making process and awaited promulgation. In addition to the rule-making proceedings, each of which portended a significant restructuring of the ways affected industries did business, there were many major investigations, studies, and cases being developed by the talented and aggressive FTC staff. Even noncognitive deception in advertising—such as cigarette advertisements containing pictures with frolicking, healthy-looking couples on a beach—was not safe from the critical eye of the FTC. George Will, a conservative columnist for the *Washington Post* observed, "The serenity of the Federal Trade Commission is hardly more secure than that of 15th century Florence, so fearful is the FTC lest some activity eligible for regulation escape regulation."

In 1984, FTC commissioner Michael Pertschuk advocates a moratorium on oil company mergers during his testimony before the House Energy and Commerce subcommittee on fossil and synthetic fuels. During Pertschuk's earlier tenure as chairman of the commission (1977–81), the FTC encountered widespread opposition as it began to announce industrywide trade regulations.

47

Some members of Congress and many businesses were alarmed at the prospect of the implementation and enforcement of these proposed rules, which would bring added costs and burdens to businesses and increased consumer awareness of rights and remedies previously unavailable to them. The potential for widespread disruptions of "business as usual" led each industry facing regulatory action to pressure Congress to do something to stop the FTC. As Senator Wendell Ford told Pertschuk, who had the misfortune of inheriting the controversial rule-making proceedings and investigations from his predecessors, "You have managed to alienate the leading citizens of every town and city in Kentucky." Senator Ford's list of FTC victims included lawyers, doctors, dentists, optometrists, funeral directors, real estate brokers, life insurance companies and salesmen, new and used car dealers, and bankers.

Perhaps the crowning blow was the initiation of an investigation and the publication in February 1978 of a proposed rule that would have regulated advertising directed at children. The children's advertising proceeding enraged the cereals industry, which enlisted a public opinion expert to assist in preserving its right to advertise sugared cereals to toddlers. The "kid vid" rule led the *Washington Post* to bestow the title of National Nanny upon the FTC.

The anti-FTC movement grew. Businesses joined forces, contributed money to political action committees (PACs), and descended in force upon Capitol Hill. In particular, the medical profession was outraged at the FTC's successful effort to attack restrictions on advertising and solicitation of patients by physicians. *FTC v. American Medical Association* (1979) was a landmark in confirming that the antitrust laws covered the professions, but it did not help the FTC on Capitol Hill.

Congressional critics joined in the attack on the commission. Representative William Frenzel railed in the House that the FTC "epitomizes all the things that Americans find excessive, unnecessary, wasteful, duplicative, and repugnant about regulatory agencies." He went on to say that "the FTC has made.itself into a virulent political and economic pestilence, insulated from the people and their representatives, and accountable to no influence except its own caprice."

Perhaps the most humiliating blow was delivered when Congress shut down the FTC for two days in May 1980 by refusing to appropriate funds for its operation because of its controversial activities. The attorney general ruled that without congressional appropriations the agency could work only to shut down its operations. Employees packed up their offices, canceled court appearances, and were called home from out-of-town investigations. The two-day closing followed a six-month battle in Congress spurred by the corporate lobbies. When the agency finally reopened, what Frenzel had termed a "king-sized cancer on the economy" had been made a virtual hostage of Congress.

Congress soon passed the FTC Improvements Act of 1980. This act prohibited the commission from promulgating any rule in any children's advertising proceeding that was based on a commission finding that such advertising was an "unfair act or practice." It also restricted the FTC's activities with respect to the standards and certification rule-making, the funeral industry rule-making, investigations of the insurance industry and agricultural cooperative practices, and trademark cancellations under the Lanham Trademark Act.

The requirement of the FTC Improvements Act of 1980 that FTC rules be subject to a two-house congressional veto was later declared unconstitutional by the courts. However, the trade regulation rules spawned during the Republican revitalization of the FTC had become the albatross of the Pertschuk chairmanship. Of the 19 rules that had been the subject of rule-making proceedings from 1975 to 1978, only 5 had been adopted in any form by the commission by 1981.

The next swing of the pendulum in the history of the FTC could have been anticipated. In September 1975, Ronald Reagan, while serving as governor of California, shared his thoughts during a conference on government regulation:

> I believe that government's principal function is to protect us from
> each other, not from ourselves. We get onto dangerous ground when
> we allow government to decide what's good for us. In the field of
> health and in the economic field, government has grown to such an
> extent that I am afraid it is showing a lack of respect for the average
> citizen. With government fostering the idea that the citizen cannot
> even buy a box of Post Toasties for himself without being cheated,
> one wonders how voters are supposed to be able to pick for govern-
> ment people who are wise enough to make all these decisions for
> them.

When he was elected president in 1980, Reagan spoke warmly about Calvin Coolidge's views on the evils of big government and Coolidge's philosophy that government that governs best governs least. Reagan chose James C. Miller III, the executive director of his Task Force on Regulatory Relief, to succeed Pertschuk as chairman of the FTC. Miller, the first economist and nonlawyer to serve as FTC chairman, was not unmindful that the commission's staff, battered but unbowed from its battles with Congress, perceived him to be the devil incarnate. On his first day at the FTC, he assembled the top-level staff,

FTC chairman James C. Miller III testifies before the House Energy and Commerce subcommittee in 1982. A disciple of the deregulation policies of President Ronald Reagan's administration, Miller cut back on many of the FTC's operations, which resulted in a decrease in the number of antitrust and consumer cases initiated by the commission.

arranged for musical accompaniment, and entered the room behind a procession of the new bureau directors and attorney advisers wearing a pair of pink plastic stick-on horns. With as much ceremonial flourish as he could muster, Miller removed his headgear and said, "I'm taking my horns off." The reaction of the assembled staff was stunned silence. Not one of them laughed.

Miller, who wore an Adam Smith tie to his confirmation hearings, became one of the principal leaders in the Reagan administration's assault on what it considered misguided and wasteful government regulation. Within weeks after he assumed office, Miller testified on Capitol Hill in favor of an FTC budget reduction for the next fiscal year.

Consumer protection enforcement declined during the Miller years. Consent orders (out-of-court settlements), a key measure of case-by-case enforcement, declined from a total of 57 in 1977 to 16 in 1983. In the antitrust arena, FTC consent orders declined from a total of 19 in 1977 to 13 in 1983, and administrative complaints dropped from 9 filed in 1977 to 1 complaint filed in

1983. Total antitrust enforcement actions declined from 42 in 1977 to 25 in 1983. Miller's FTC did aggressively preserve the commission's authority to regulate the professions. Its action against the Indiana Federation of Dentists was upheld by the Supreme Court. However, the FTC's infrequent exercise of its prosecutorial powers left much to be desired by the public-interest bar.

Miller promoted the view that the best consumer protection possible is provided by an efficient marketplace. Little or no government intervention was necessary, reasoned Miller, so long as consumers had enough information for them to act reasonably. Consistent with that view—which ignored consumers who were gullible, forgetful, did not subscribe to *Consumer Reports*, or did not keep up with the mass media—Miller wrote a letter to Representative John Dingell, chairman of the powerful Subcommittee on Oversight and Investigation of the House Commerce Committee in October 1983, setting forth the FTC's policy on deceptive acts and practices. The letter, which asserted that consumers should act more reasonably to avoid being hurt in the marketplace, was denounced by some observers as flawed in its legal reasoning and was rejected by the committee.

The Miller regime at the FTC was also driven by faith in cost-benefit analysis. President Reagan adopted an executive order that compelled regulatory officials to choose the least costly way of achieving a regulatory goal. If a regulation would impose more costs than benefits, it would not be adopted. This position ignored the fact that some of these costly regulations were necessary in order to protect certain rights guaranteed by law.

To fill the void in enforcement left by the FTC, some state attorneys general stepped in to prosecute cases brought under state statutes, which are modeled after the FTC Act and known as "Little FTC Acts." As a result of what Professor Milton Handler has called "the vigorous and effective non-enforcement of the antitrust laws," the National Association of Attorneys General, an organization of state attorneys general, issued its own merger guidelines in 1987 that made it easier for the states to challenge large takeovers. Five mergers approved by the FTC and the Department of Justice have been successfully challenged by the states. Following a policy of noninterference in economic affairs, federal regulators of the 1980s and their business allies suddenly recognized a new enemy: Unrestrained state action could produce a crazy quilt of dissimilar state laws and regulations that could severely restrict interstate commerce.

Miller left the FTC in 1985 to become director of the OMB. He was succeeded briefly by commissioner Terry Calvani, who served as acting chairman of the FTC, and then by Daniel Oliver, who was sworn in on April 21,

1986. Oliver, a former law professor, believed that government was the principal source of impediments to free competition. The Oliver policy was to rely on the "competitive motivations of industry members" for the effectiveness of the FTC's antitrust remedies. Oliver viewed the increasing prevalence of hostile takeovers as a means of disciplining inefficient corporate managers rather than a reason to intervene with an FTC challenge to a merger. He also believed that the marketplace was the best regulator of advertising.

Oliver described the state attorneys general as "counterrevolutionaries" who were "a threat to our basic constitutional scheme." The Supreme Court did not agree. In *Reiter v. Sonotone* (1979), the Court had upheld the right of state attorneys general to sue for recovery of damages suffered by consumers. In *California v. ARC America* (1989), the Court rejected the argument that federal antitrust laws should preempt the application of state laws. "Congress," said the Court, "intended the federal antitrust laws to supplement, not displace, state antitrust remedies." When asked what he considered to be his greatest achievements as chairman, Oliver replied, "What does a deregulator put on his resume? I guess you list the cases you did not bring." True to his goal, the FTC's 1987 Annual Report noted that "the Commission advanced the policies underlying its Congressional mandate, through cost-effective non-enforcement activities."

In early 1989, staff morale, already battered by the agency's lowered profile, deteriorated further when another reduction in force resulted in the firing of experienced staffers. By the end of the Reagan administration, the entire FTC staff had shrunk to under 900, about half the size that it was in 1981. As New York attorney general Robert Abrams put it, the FTC had become "the watchdog put to sleep."

As the Bush administration was getting under way, the ABA's Section of Antitrust Law released a report by a special committee that it appointed to study the role of the FTC. The committee—headed by Miles W. Kirkpatrick, who had headed a similar ABA study group 20 years earlier—found that the FTC's role remained ill defined. The special committee suggested that the commission do more to articulate its advertising law enforcement agenda, saw few opportunities for broad rule-making, and noted that the drastic cuts in the FTC's staff was cause for serious concern. The committee urged better use of available resources and that an increase in overall FTC resources should be provided.

President George Bush appointed Janet Steiger, a self-described "nonlawyer, noneconomist, and non-man," as the first woman to chair the FTC. Steiger, a close friend of the president's and the former chairman of the Postal

During his confirmation hearing for the FTC chairmanship in August 1970, Miles W. Kirkpatrick answers questions before the Senate Commerce Committee. In 1969 and 1989, Kirkpatrick headed American Bar Association committees that conducted detailed investigations of the FTC. Both studies pointed out the deficiencies of the commission and recommended improvements.

Rate Commission, was sworn in on August 11, 1989. Steiger has adopted a more aggressive FTC agenda than her Republican predecessors and has moved to repair the FTC's relations with Congress. With the end of the antiregulatory 1980s, the FTC staff and many FTC watchers are hoping that the agency is headed toward a revival.

Attorneys in the Office of the General Counsel discuss an FTC project that involves the cooperation of state law enforcement authorities. The FTC attempts to ensure compliance with the laws that it enforces by fostering voluntary cooperation from businesses and by pursuing formal administrative cases against alleged violators.

FOUR

Inside the Commission

When it passed the FTC Act in 1914, Congress assigned several tasks to the new agency it created. As Woodrow Wilson envisioned it, the FTC would prepare studies and reports on activities in the marketplace that would inform the public, Congress, and the commission itself. The FTC would also act as a guardian of the marketplace, investigating conduct that might violate the laws it enforced and, when the facts required, issuing complaints alleging violations of the law. After a formal fact-finding process, the commissioners would then render a decision and, if appropriate, issue a cease and desist order.

Today the FTC conducts even more of the activities than it originally was authorized to pursue and has retained many of the same procedures that developed in the early days of its operations. Although its authority and responsibility have been enlarged by Congress over the years, it retains the same core objectives that characterized its early days.

The Commissioners

At the top of the FTC's hierarchy are the five commissioners, each of whom is nominated by the president and confirmed by the Senate. The president designates one of the commissioners as chairman of the agency. Under the FTC Act, no more than three of the five commissioners may belong to the same political party. Each commissioner is appointed for a seven-year term, but a replacement commissioner may be appointed to complete a term in the event of a vacancy. Commissioners may be reappointed to another term, again with the advice and consent of the Senate. Other than the appointment and confirmation processes and the power to impeach, the president and Congress do not exert any direct control over the actions of the FTC commissioners. However, they indirectly control the commission through the budget and appropriation process. Also, various congressional committees are empowered to hold oversight hearings to ensure that the FTC is carrying out the intent of the legislation that it enforces.

Although the chairman has just one vote at commission meetings, in reality he or she exercises considerable influence on FTC operations and policies. The chairman controls the executive and administrative functions of the agency and appoints the bureau directors, the general counsel, and the executive director. Because these are among the most powerful positions in the agency, the chairman may, through these appointees, strongly influence the philosophy and

The FTC commissioners pause during one of their meetings in 1990. The commissioners vote on a wide variety of matters, including whether to authorize an investigation, to issue an administrative complaint, or to accept or reject a consent agreement. The commissioners also make final decisions in cases that are litigated before the commission.

direction of the commission. The chairman also appoints the FTC staff within the limits of civil service protections.

Some meetings of the commission are open to the public, but most are closed. For example, because law enforcement investigations are nonpublic, FTC meetings at which the commissioners consider the issuance of a complaint charging violations of the law are routinely closed. Before the meeting, matters to be discussed may be placed on the agenda by any of the commissioners. Decisions may be made at the meeting by voice vote; however, most are resolved by written motions circulated by individual commissioners. If there is a tie vote, no action is taken. The commissioners vote on a wide variety of matters, including

- The decision to begin a rule-making proceeding or to promulgate a final rule.
- The initiation of an industrywide investigation.
- The authorization of the use of the FTC's compulsory process power to issue subpoenas or civil investigative demands in connection with an investigation.
- The issuance of administrative complaints.
- A decision to accept or reject a consent agreement.

As in many other regulatory agencies, the same five commissioners who authorize an investigation and initiate a prosecution by issuing a complaint also make the final decision in cases that are litigated administratively.

Each commissioner has a small staff consisting of an assistant and attorney and economic advisers. The advisers, generally selected from the ranks of FTC staff attorneys and economists, review matters referred to the commission in order to advise their commissioner on what action would be appropriate and legally sound. In addition to advisers, the chairman's office includes an assistant to the chairman and an executive assistant to the chairman. Because of the chairman's powerful administrative role at the FTC, these two staffers enjoy broad powers and often are regarded as the eyes and ears of the chairman.

Office of the Executive Director

The executive director is the FTC's central management and administrative official. He or she is responsible for providing support services and advice related to personnel, budget and finance, procurements, computers, management information, and the library. The executive director also supervises the

A staff member of the FTC's Office of Public Affairs (right) answers a question in the commission's public reference room. In addition to replying to requests for information from the public, the Office of Public Affairs develops press releases and responds to inquiries from the press.

10 regional offices and helps integrate their operations with headquarters's activities. The executive director develops the agency's budget and searches for methods to economize the FTC's financial resources.

The Public Reference Section maintains a wide variety of consumer information materials authored by the FTC staff on subjects ranging from warranty and credit rights to when to ask a grocer for a rain check if an advertised special is unavailable. It also supplies detailed guides to businesses to help them comply with laws enforced by the FTC.

Office of the General Counsel

The general counsel serves as the FTC's chief legal adviser. Attorneys in the Office of the General Counsel provide legal guidance to the commissioners and interact with a wide variety of local, state, and federal officials. They give advice concerning the FTC's Rules of Practice, deal with requests for agency records under the Freedom of Information Act, and handle all appeals of FTC decisions in federal courts of appeal.

The work of the general counsel is separate and distinct from that of the prosecutors in the FTC's operating bureaus, the Bureau of Competition and the Bureau of Consumer Protection. Bureau attorneys advocate particular positions on matters before the commission; however, they are prohibited from contacting the commissioners concerning matters that are being litigated administratively within the FTC.

Unlike many federal agencies, the FTC has authority to represent itself in numerous cases before the lower federal courts rather than having to be represented by attorneys from the Department of Justice. If the Department of Justice declines to do so, the FTC may represent itself before the Supreme Court. In 1989, for example, Ernest J. Isenstadt, the assistant general counsel for litigation, argued the FTC's case against the D.C. Superior Court Trial Lawyers Association before the Supreme Court.

Office of the Secretary

The FTC also has a secretary, who is responsible for signing all commission orders and official correspondence. The Office of the Secretary also receives

General Counsel James M. Spears (left) discusses a legal issue with two staff members. The general counsel, the FTC's chief legal adviser, and his staff provide neutral legal counsel to the FTC commissioners and other government officials.

filings from parties to formal and informal proceedings before the agency, serves all official documents issued by the commission and its administrative judges, creates official minutes recording all commission deliberations and decisions, serves as intermediary between the FTC and its staff, and receives and processes all communications from Congress.

Office of Congressional Relations

The Office of Congressional Relations coordinates the FTC's efforts to inform and work with Congress. It monitors proposed legislation and coordinates the presentation of testimony by commissioners and FTC staff members before congressional committees.

Office of Public Affairs

The Office of Public Affairs is responsible for developing press releases that announce the commission's actions and responds to inquiries from the media. This office publishes a weekly calendar and a news summary, prepares outlines of other matters not covered by news releases, and responds to requests for information from the public.

Office of Consumer and Competition Advocacy

The Office of Consumer and Competition Advocacy coordinates the FTC's efforts to inform other governmental and self-regulatory agencies about the potential effects of proposed legislation and rules on consumers. In fiscal year 1990, the FTC staff submitted 40 comments and briefs covering a variety of topics to other agencies and groups.

Operating Bureaus

Below the chairman and the commissioners, the substantive work of the FTC is divided among its three operating bureaus: the Bureau of Competition, the Bureau of Consumer Protection, and the Bureau of Economics. More than 90 percent of the FTC's budget is devoted to the activities of these bureaus. The Bureau of Competition is primarily responsible for recommending FTC action to prevent unfair methods of competition and to promote competition through the enforcement of the FTC Act and federal antitrust laws such as the Clayton Act. The Bureau of Consumer Protection recommends FTC action to eliminate unfair or deceptive acts or practices, particularly those that unreasonably restrict or inhibit consumer choices in the marketplace. The Bureau of Economics provides economic analysis for the FTC's antitrust and consumer protection activities, advises the commission on the likely effects of government regulation and restraints on competition, and gathers and analyzes information on the U.S. economy and the domestic marketplace.

Bureau of Competition

The Bureau of Competition is charged with preventing business practices that restrain competition through its antitrust law enforcement efforts and by appearing before other government agencies to advocate free-market policies. The bureau carries out its enforcement responsibilities by investigating allegations that the law has been violated and, when appropriate, recommending that the FTC either file a lawsuit in federal district court seeking an injunction, initiating litigation before an administrative law judge by filing a

Attorneys in the Bureau of Competition's general litigation division discuss a merger case. By assisting in the enforcement of antitrust laws, the Bureau of Competition seeks to prohibit trade practices that restrain competition.

formal complaint, entering into a consent agreement (an out-of-court settlement), or beginning an investigation to determine whether an existing FTC order is being violated.

As of December 1990, the Bureau of Competition employed 154 lawyers. They work in different divisions within the bureau. The divisions are organized under several senior managers who report to the bureau director. Among the divisions are

- The premerger notification office, which handles the initial review of proposed merger transactions.
- The mergers division, which investigates all types of mergers and acquisitions.
- The energy and food division, which handles cases involving oil, gas, food, and grocery stores.
- The professions, or licensed occupations, division, which focuses primarily on anticompetitive practices of licensing boards and trade and professional associations.
- The health care division, which addresses anticompetitive practices and mergers in the medical care and services sector and also handles some real estate matters.

The Bureau of Competition also has a task force that focuses on nonmerger cases involving horizontal and vertical restraints and Robinson-Patman Act violations. The bureau's Compliance Division monitors obedience with FTC competition orders, drafts rules regarding the premerger notification requirements of the HSR Act, and brings cases against companies that fail to comply with FTC orders or the premerger notification requirements of the HSR Act.

The bureau's most time- and work-intensive activity occurs within the premerger notification program. Before the HSR Act was passed, the FTC and the Department of Justice challenged acquisitions of companies only after the merger had been completed. The remedy of divestiture (an order requiring a merger to be dissolved) often came many years after the merger had been accomplished. Today most mergers are challenged before they are executed. Because divestiture of the acquired company is so expensive, many times the mere threat of FTC action against a merger is enough to stop it. For example, in May 1988, McCormick & Company, a spice company, abandoned its plan to acquire another company in the same business, Spice Islands, after the FTC voted unanimously to authorize the staff to seek a preliminary injunction blocking the merger. Had the merger gone through, the FTC estimated that the combined companies would have controlled 80 percent of the market in gourmet spices.

The premerger notification program requires firms to report most impending mergers to the FTC and the Department of Justice so those agencies can determine whether a particular proposed merger might violate the antitrust laws. With the aid of economists, staff attorneys determine whether the proposed merger fits within the guidelines published by the FTC and the Department of Justice. At the FTC, a preliminary review takes place within a week after the notification documents are filed.

After receiving a premerger notification, the staff prepares a summary description of the proposed transaction and a preliminary antitrust analysis. In essence, the staff tries to define the market(s) within which the firms operate both in terms of geographic area and the product(s) sold. The staff then scrutinizes the level of concentration in the market—that is, the number of firms that operate in the market and what percentage of the sales are made by each firm. The staff uses the Herfindahl-Hirschman Index, a mathematical method of measuring market concentration, to ascertain whether a few firms sell a large percentage of the total number of products sold by that industry.

The staff then concludes whether, as a result of the proposed merger, the newly merged company will be able to raise prices without worrying about competition from existing competitors or new entrants in that market. The staff considers the likelihood that a new firm would enter the industry and become a competitor within two years if the proposed merger were to be permitted. A number of barriers—including the high cost of advertising, the reputation of existing firms with consumers, the lack of shelf space, the need to construct new facilities, and the cost of complying with government regulations—may prevent or delay new entrants from gaining a foothold in the market. If entry into the market is easy, existing firms will be reluctant to raise prices above a competitive level because higher prices will attract new competitors. In such cases, the FTC is less likely to challenge the merger as anticompetitive. The FTC in recent years has blocked efforts by Coca-Cola to acquire Dr. Pepper and an effort by Pepsico to acquire 7-Up.

Not all of the enforcement actions within the Bureau of Competition involve mergers. A special unit within one division has been designated to examine nonmerger restraint of trade cases such as those involving so-called horizontal combinations. Agreements in which sellers who supposedly compete against each other instead conspire to fix prices or agree to restrain the volume of goods they will sell in order to lessen competition are considered anticompetitive. In the past, the bureau's horizontal restraints program has focused on the health care industry, in which increases in costs have outpaced inflation. During fiscal year 1989, the FTC took action against a group of physicians who pressured other doctors who had agreed to work for a health maintenance organization (HMO). The staff also evaluated allegations of anticompetitive rules and regulations enforced by state licensing boards and private professional and trade associations. In addition, the FTC issued a decision and order against the Detroit Auto Dealers Association, which had agreed to restrict the hours that member dealers would be open for business.

The Bureau of Competition also reviews claims of anticompetitive practices in the distribution of goods from manufacturers to consumers and monitors compliance with the Robinson-Patman Act. Other potentially anticompetitive practices examined by the FTC staff include refusals of manufacturers to deal with particular distributors, dealer terminations, efforts to interfere with a competitor's supply of products, and agreements that prevent or restrict other companies from competing in the marketplace. During fiscal year 1989, the FTC staff also continued an ongoing administrative litigation against six major book publishers over allegations that certain pricing practices violate the Robinson-Patman Act. The Bureau of Competition also remains on the lookout for single firms that have sufficient market power within an industry to reduce output below or increase prices above a competitive level.

Bureau of Consumer Protection

The Bureau of Consumer Protection is charged with stopping or preventing unfair or deceptive practices that injure consumers and restrain free and fair competition. It promotes increased consumer information and the use of truthful advertising that allows consumers to make informed choices when they purchase goods and services. The bureau staff also works to reduce market-place restrictions that inflate prices and limit the availability of goods and services, and it plays a major role in preventing creditors and debt collectors from using unlawful practices. It also polices companies that fail to honor product warranties and performance and reliability claims.

The work of the Bureau of Consumer Protection is divided among half a dozen programs and, as of December 1990, was carried out by 133 lawyers. For example, the Division of Marketing Practices, the largest program, focuses on bringing cases under the FTC trade regulation rules that were promulgated in the 1970s, including the franchise rule and the funeral rule. This division also handles cases alleging the use of unfair or deceptive marketing practices.

James J. Cutler (right), director of the Bureau of Consumer Protection, reviews a pending case with Julia Oas, a staff attorney. The Bureau of Consumer Protection is responsible for preventing the use of unfair or deceptive advertising and marketing practices. It also enforces a number of specific consumer laws, such as the Wool Products Labeling Act and the Consumer Credit Protection Act.

Over the years the staff of the Division of Marketing Practices has achieved some significant victories against fraud. Since 1972, the FTC has issued 12 final orders against land developers who misrepresented the purchase of their land as a sound financial investment involving little risk. Often the homesites, located on desert land in Arizona, New Mexico, California, and Colorado or in swampy subdivisions in undesirable parts of Florida, were sold to potential retirees. In the first such case against GAC Corporation, a vice-president of the corporation attempted to justify the company's practices after the issuance of the FTC's complaint by stating on national television that some people really liked underwater land because they could fish on it.

The Marketing Practices program in recent years has also gone after telemarketing fraud involving investment coins and art, mineral leasing, consumer goods, travel, and other goods and services. Typically, these cases involve deceptive sales pitches about the investment value of a product made over the telephone lines of a phone bank set up in an office. The telemarketing fraud investigations initiated by the FTC between 1983 and 1990 produced injunctions against 212 defendants, judgments of more than $148 million, and consumer redress of more than $58 million.

Recent rule-making activities in the Division of Marketing Practices included a proposed amendment to the franchise rule. The amendment, if adopted, would require franchisers to provide additional disclosures concerning aspects of the operation of the business (including cost and earnings information) to potential franchise purchasers. For example, franchisers such as McDonald's would have to provide the additional information to those who are considering the purchase of a franchise to operate an individual McDonald's restaurant.

The Division of Marketing Practices also handles cases involving enforcement of the warranty provisions of the Magnuson-Moss Act. This act requires manufacturers and sellers of consumer products to provide purchasers with information about warranty terms and conditions at the point of sale. FTC attorneys monitor compliance with the act and inform consumers about their warranty rights in FTC pamphlets. The FTC has traditionally been concerned

C. Lee Peeler (right), associate director for Advertising Practices, watches a staff attorney's demonstration of the Gut-Buster, an exercise product. The FTC was instrumental in having the Gut-Buster pulled off the market because it inflicted injuries on users.

with the warranties issued by manufacturers of major consumer products, such as cars, appliances, and mobile homes. That concern led to promulgation of the used-car rule, which requires that notices be placed on used cars for sale that indicate whether or not they are sold "as is" (without a warranty) or with a full or limited warranty.

The Advertising Practices Division is the second largest program within the Bureau of Consumer Protection. Advertising constitutes the most important source of information for consumers about the products and services that they buy. Untruthful advertising not only misleads consumers but also harms honest competitors. The courts have ruled that an advertiser must have a reasonable basis for any claims made about product performance before making the claims.

The FTC's advertising practices program is divided into four sections that monitor general advertising, tobacco advertising, food and drug advertising, and energy advertising. The 17 attorneys in the Advertising Practices Division monitor advertising that appears on television and in magazines and newspapers in search of potential targets of FTC enforcement efforts. For example, the FTC filed a complaint against the Campbell Soup Company, alleging that certain Campbell advertisements linked the low-fat and low-cholesterol content of Campbell soups with a reduced risk of some forms of heart disease without disclosing that the soups are high in sodium and that diets high in sodium may increase the risk of heart disease. In another case, General Nutrition Corporation was required to pay $600,000 for research and to stop making false and unsubstantiated claims about its products after the FTC charged that the company made unsubstantiated claims that its diet supplement, "Healthy Greens," would reduce the risk of cancer. In June 1990, the FTC accepted a consent agreement prohibiting the maker of Mazola Corn Oil and Mazola Margarine from misrepresenting the effect of those products on serum cholesterol levels.

The FTC has been a leader in the fight against misleading tobacco advertisements. In 1989, the R. J. Reynolds Tobacco Company agreed to settle charges that its "Of Cigarettes and Science" ad campaign, although presented in the style of an editorial, was an advertisement that misrepresented a scientific study on the health effects of smoking. Reynolds agreed not to misrepresent the purpose or results of studies in any discussion of cigarette smoking and health effects in the future. It also agreed to disclose in any future advertising discussing the study that the government study concluded that those who quit smoking are less at risk of coronary disease than those who continue to smoke.

All irons should come with this seal. Only one does.

Only the Black & Decker Automatic Shut-Off™ iron shuts off and stays off.

Other automatic shut-off irons can reheat if knocked over.

But not the Black & Decker Automatic Shut-Off™ iron. It beeps to warn you it's been left on, then shuts itself off. And stays off, even if knocked over.

So buy the only iron endorsed by the National Fire Safety Council. And get the features that not only make ironing simpler, but give you peace of mind as well.

BLACK & DECKER
IDEAS AT WORK.™

The FTC responded to this advertisement for Black & Decker's Automatic Shut-Off Iron by pursuing a complaint against the company, alleging that the National Fire Safety Council lacked expertise in evaluating or testing appliance fire safety and that it did not grant its exclusive endorsement to Black & Decker. In 1989, Black & Decker entered into a consent agreement with the FTC, agreeing not to misrepresent the nature of endorsements of any of its products, including the iron.

The FTC is only one component of a network of advertising regulatory mechanisms. Before an advertisement appears on network television, it must be approved by censors at the major networks who look for deceptive claims or misleading comparisons. Matthew Margo, vice-president for program practices at CBS, told the *Washington Post* that of the 50,000 product advertisements submitted to CBS for approval in 1989, about a third had to be revised or substantiated. Unfortunately, the cable television industry does not have an advertising-screening procedure similar to that utilized by the major networks. It is only after objectional ads get on the air that consumers and competitors complain to the FTC, a state attorney general, or the advertising industry's own National Advertising Division of the Better Business Bureaus, Inc. In 1989, the National Advertising Division reviewed 104 complaints and negotiated agreements with advertisers to modify or discontinue the advertisements in 76 of those cases.

The ABA's special committee that studied the FTC in 1989 was particularly concerned about whether the FTC was prosecuting its fair share of significant advertising cases. The number of advertising enforcement actions has varied between 12 and 20 annually during the 1980s. During fiscal year 1989, the Advertising Practices staff secured only nine consent orders, filed three administrative complaints, and secured a small number of preliminary injunctions. However, the work-hours that the FTC devoted to advertising declined by one-third between 1978 and 1990. On a more positive note, the FTC has won every advertising case it has litigated since 1980, which may be a sign of better case selection or an aversion to pursuing big, challenging cases. Critics have noted that of the 25 complaints issued against advertisers from 1984 to 1988, 12 involved diet or health supplements, baldness cures, and tanning devices, whereas only 6 challenged network television advertisements, and 4 of those cases involved air or water cleaners. However, in 1989, the FTC filed complaints against Kraft, Inc., Reynolds Tobacco, Campbell Soup Company, and Revlon—hardly the small, fly-by-night companies.

The FTC has tended to avoid bringing cases challenging deceptive advertising for products that are commonly available, inexpensive, and purchased repeatedly by a consumer. The FTC's failure to act in those cases may be attributed to its unwillingness to spend scarce resources on such cases, based on its theory that a reasonable consumer can figure out when he or she is being duped by advertisements for frequently purchased products.

For claims that are obvious or clearly implied in the advertisement, the FTC can use its expertise to determine what consumers are led to believe and whether the representations are false or deceptive. For example, in a 1975

In 1986, the FTC issued a complaint charging the R. J. Reynolds Tobacco Company with making false and misleading claims in its "Of Cigarettes and Science" advertisements. The commission and R. J. Reynolds settled the charges by entering into a consent agreement in 1989.

case that the FTC litigated against Warner-Lambert Co., an administrative law judge (ALJ) issued an order forbidding the company from advertising that Listerine mouthwash killed germs that cause colds and sore throats and ordered the firm to engage in corrective advertising for two years. The case was appealed to the commission, which affirmed the ALJ's decision and ordered Warner-Lambert to spend $10 million to correct consumer misimpressions concerning Listerine.

The Bureau of Consumer Protection's Credit Practices program pursues deceptive or unfair credit-related practices that seriously injure consumers. The staff enforces a variety of laws—including the Consumer Credit Protection Act, parts of the Truth-in-Lending Act, and the Fair Debt Collection Practices Act—to ensure that consumers know the true cost of the credit they receive and that collection practices are not unfair or deceptive. The credit practices staff also monitors compliance with the Equal Credit Opportunity Act and the Fair Credit Reporting Act, which assure that women, minorities, and the elderly have equal access to credit and that credit-reporting companies accurately report information about credit history.

In recent years, the credit practices program has focused on misleading or fraudulent claims by companies that sell credit repair services and by firms that claim to procure credit cards for those with bad credit records. In one case, two former officials of Credit-Rite agreed to settle FTC charges that they misrepresented their ability to improve consumers' credit bureau reports and their intentions to make refunds. As a result of criminal charges filed by the U.S. Attorney's Office in New Jersey, both of the defendants were ordered to pay restitution, and one was sentenced to a prison term. In fiscal year 1989, complaints filed in credit practices cases in federal district courts resulted in $3,756,000 in consumer redress and $360,000 in civil penalties.

The Division of Service Industry Practices has recently focused on investment fraud and fraud in the advertising and promotion of health care diagnostic and treatment services, such as infertility treatments. The staff has litigated against those who sold allegedly valuable coins that were not very valuable, contracts for gold, and phony Salvador Dali artworks. Since 1983, the division has filed suit in connection with 29 alleged investment frauds, obtained orders against 179 investment fraud defendants and judgments of more than $98 million, and secured consumer redress for scam victims of more than $62 million.

The Enforcement Program of the Bureau of Consumer Protection enforces FTC orders and rules and ensures that required compliance reports are filed by those subject to outstanding FTC orders. In fiscal year 1990, the FTC obtained

$2.4 million in civil penalties for violations, including $100,000 from a funeral casket company that violated an FTC order entered in 1941. The staff seeks to remedy violations of the law by asking the Department of Justice to go to court to obtain civil penalties for violations of FTC rules and orders, injunctions, and, when supported by evidence of economic loss, consumer redress. Recently, the Enforcement Program has sought cash reimbursement and product repair or replacement under FTC orders. It also has given thousands of owners of General Motors and Volkswagen cars a chance to resolve their car problems through the mediation program of the National Council of Better Business Bureaus. More than $62 million has been paid out, in refunds and repairs, to General Motors customers alone.

The Office of Consumer and Business Education encourages informed consumer choice by developing consumer and business education pamphlets based on staff investigations that unearth marketplace problems and demonstrate a need for increased consumer information. The FTC has a "best sellers" list of publications, including Spanish translations, on topics ranging from how to comply with the used-car rule to how to care for clothes covered by the care labeling rule. More attention will be devoted to consumer education in the future.

Bureau of Economics

The Bureau of Economics serves as the economic adviser to the commission and provides economic analysis to support the casework and rule-making proceedings brought by the Bureau of Competition and the Bureau of Consumer Protection. As part of its Antitrust Policy Analysis Program in fiscal year 1989, the Bureau of Economics studied potential entry by pipelines in the natural gas markets, hospital mergers, hospital rate regulation, concentration in grocery retailing, and the market effects of the FTC's decisions not to challenge certain mergers. The bureau published staff reports on the cost of sham litigation, mergers in the U.S. petroleum industry, and trade restrictions on textiles, steel, and automobiles.

On the consumer protection side, the Bureau of Economics initiated several studies of consumer-related issues, including the effects of health-claims advertising on the consumption of fat and cholesterol, airline advertising, and consumer attitudes toward brands of food that do not disclose nutritional information. The bureau published reports on health claims in the advertising of fiber cereals, health claims in advertising generally, state regulations, intrastate long-distance telephone rates, and local building codes.

John L. Peterman (right), director of the Bureau of Economics, examines a case with three other FTC administrators. The Bureau of Economics serves as an adviser to the commission and provides economic analysis to support cases brought by the Bureau of Competition and the Bureau of Consumer Protection.

Regional Offices

The FTC's 10 regional offices are located in Atlanta, Boston, Chicago, Cleveland, Dallas, Denver, Los Angeles, New York, San Francisco, and Seattle. These offices function as mini-FTCs for their regions and bring cases that cover the full range of FTC enforcement concerns, although consumer protection cases are emphasized. They maintain ongoing relationships with officials of state and local governments on matters of common interest. Because of their presence in the field, the regional offices are sometimes perceived to be subject to more local political pressures.

During the FTC's low-profile Reagan years of retrenchment, the regional offices played a more active role. Perhaps because they were removed from the day-to-day scrutiny of the headquarters staff and the commissioners, the regional offices opened approximately 43 percent of all FTC investigations during the period from 1981 to 1988, and regional office work years increased 12 percent from 1987 to 1988.

A staff member in the FTC's Los Angeles regional office fields a telephone inquiry. The regional offices, which receive hundreds of inquiries each week, function as the principal liaison between local consumers and the FTC.

FIVE

The Tools of Regulation

Congress gave the FTC several tools to carry out its two basic mandates: to protect consumers and to enforce the antitrust laws. These tools include the power to write reports about economic conditions and business practices, to prosecute violations of the law, and to make law by promulgating industrywide rules.

How the FTC Learns of Possible Violations of the Law

The FTC staff has many different sources of information that may lead to an informal or, if necessary, a formal investigation. The agency receives letters from consumers who have been harmed by a consumer product or business practice, and businesses also write to complain about the practices of their competitors. However, because the FTC generally does not intervene in individual cases and can only act in the public interest, the staff must focus on practices that generate repeated and widespread complaints.

A good place to learn about potential violations of the law is in the trade press, where stories about individual companies describe company plans,

Two attorneys in the Advertising Practices Division discuss a case involving the Norelco Clean Water Machine. To protect consumers from false or deceptive marketing practices, the Advertising Practices staff monitors television programs, magazines, and newspapers for advertising claims that seem too good to be true.

advertising campaigns, and industry practices. The FTC staffers assigned to programs that follow a particular industry subscribe to those publications and read them regularly. The Advertising Practices Division staff monitors television programs, magazines, and newspapers for advertising claims that seem too good to be true. Other consumer protection staffers get ideas from their friends, their families, and their own experiences as consumers. On the antitrust side, the mergers staff has more than enough information from the premerger notification filings required by the HSR Act to keep it busy, but it does keep an eye on the healthy pace of mergers and acquisitions through the *Wall Street Journal* and other sources of business news. Even the FTC's economists contribute ideas for enforcement actions based on what they learn from their industry studies.

The FTC staff may investigate a matter informally without the approval of the commission by asking for information over the telephone and checking public records maintained by other agencies. These informal investigations are conducted to decide whether to initiate a formal investigation that would require a significant commitment of FTC resources. If an investigation will probe the practices of an entire industry, the commission may announce the investigation by issuing a press release. If an investigation will focus on a particular firm, the investigation generally will not be made public unless the firm files a motion to quash compulsory process, a formal complaint is issued that charges the firm with a violation of law, or a consent settlement is reached and approved by the commission.

The Exercise of Prosecutorial Discretion

In order to open an investigation of a company, an industry, or an individual, an FTC staff member must obtain the approval of the appropriate bureau director, and if the investigation requires the use of the FTC's power to compel the submission of documents and testimony by issuing a subpoena or a civil investigative demand, the commission itself must issue a resolution authorizing the use of compulsory process. Prior to the issuance of such a resolution by the commission, the staff prepares a memorandum summarizing the reasons for the initiation of a formal investigation and why compulsory process is necessary, based on the information the staff acquired during its informal investigation.

In deciding whether to open a formal investigation, the FTC staff considers the importance of the product to consumers, the cost of the product, what

A staff attorney (left) and an investigator confer on a case in the FTC's Los Angeles regional office. The FTC staff may conduct informal investigations to determine whether the commission should initiate a formal investigation into potentially illegal conduct.

evidence the staff has that the alleged practice is widespread, or if the investigation is to focus on the practices of a single firm, if there is any evidence of a pattern of unfair, deceptive, or anticompetitive behavior. The staff also analyzes, on a preliminary basis, whether what it believes is occurring in the marketplace may be illegal. In the Bureau of Competition, investigations of agreements among businesses that compete at the same level (such as General Motors and Ford) that may restrain trade are classified loosely as "horizontal restraints," and agreements among businesses that operate at different levels of the distribution chain (such as manufacturers and dealers) are called "vertical restraints."

Several types of horizontal restraints, such as agreements to fix prices or to divide up market territories, are generally seen by the courts as per se (automatic) violations of the law because they almost always injure competition by increasing prices or reducing output. Vertical restraints might include resale price maintenance, restrictions on the territory in which a dealer may sell, restrictions on customers with whom a distributor can deal, and agreements requiring the purchase of more than one item. In general, the courts apply a "rule of reason" analysis to nonprice vertical restraints by balancing the procompetitive and anticompetitive effects of the restraints. To determine whether a restrictive practice should be prohibited as imposing an unreasonable restraint on competition, the Supreme Court has said:

> The court must ordinarily consider the facts peculiar to the business to which the restraint is applied; its condition before and after the restraint was imposed; the nature of the restraint and its effect, actual or probable. The history of the restraint, the evil believed to exist, the reason for adopting the particular remedy, the purpose or end sought to be attained, are all relevant facts.

In merger cases the staff usually consults, in addition to federal court and FTC decisions, various official guidelines, such as the 1984 Department of Justice merger guidelines, the FTC's 1982 Statement Concerning Horizontal Mergers, and, in appropriate cases, the Department of Justice's 1988 Antitrust Enforcement Guidelines for International Operations.

Based on the information set forth in the premerger notification filing and the evidence gathered as a result of its second request, the Bureau of Competition staff decides whether the characteristics of the industry, including entry barriers, suggest that the proposed merger would present competitive concerns. The staff tries to predict whether a new competitor would be likely to enter the market within two years. If the proposed merger appears to be anticompetitive, the staff then must decide whether there is an acceptable remedy and what that remedy might be. One possibility might be a settlement that would resolve the risks to competition uncovered by the investigation. The Bureau of Competition has used such novel remedies as licensing of competitors to produce a product and divestitures of trademarks and customer and supplier lists. Alternatively, the staff might recommend that the FTC seek an injunction in court to block the transaction immediately.

In 1980, the FTC issued an "unfairness" policy statement in response to congressional concern that the FTC's jurisdiction over unfair acts and practices in the consumer protection area was too broad. The commission's unfairness policy statement identified the criteria it uses to determine whether a particular act or practice should be forbidden on the ground that it is "unfair." It said, in essence, an unfair act or practice is one that causes substantial consumer injury that is not outweighed by any offsetting consumer or competitive benefits and that consumers cannot reasonably avoid.

The Threat of Government Action

Because lawsuits have become expensive, mounting a full-scale defense of a major antitrust case or even a consumer protection action can cost hundreds of thousands of dollars. Thus, the mere threat of government action may cause the parties to a merger transaction to modify or abandon their plans. For example, the parties may enter into a consent decree with the FTC in which the agency agrees not to pursue an enforcement action in return for a promise of the parties to a merger to divest themselves of certain assets or product lines. When KKR Associates acquired RJR Nabisco in a celebrated merger in 1989, the FTC required KKR to divest certain product lines.

On the consumer protection side, the mere announcement that the FTC has instituted an industrywide investigation of certain practices may be enough to persuade responsible businesses to abandon questionable practices. Shortly after an industrywide investigation of time-sharing vacation plans was announced in the late 1970s, the operators of a computerized service that matched owners of time-share vacation units who wished to exchange their time-shares for a vacation elsewhere sought a meeting with the FTC staff to learn how to improve their business practices to avoid becoming a subject of an investigation.

What Happens During an Investigation

The objective of an investigation is for the staff to determine whether prosecutable violations of the laws administered by the FTC have occurred. After the commission issues a resolution authorizing the use of compulsory process in an investigation, the staff may seek the voluntary production of evidence, or it may request the commission's permission to issue subpoenas or civil investigative demands to those who are thought to have information needed in the investigation. The commission may issue *subpoenas duces tecum* (for documents and other objects of evidence) or *subpoenas ad testificandum* (for testimony). The subpoenas may require individuals to appear and testify in investigational hearings (depositions) that are held before a presiding official (generally an FTC attorney). At the investigational hearings, witnesses testify under oath and are questioned by an FTC staff attorney. A witness may, if he or she chooses, be represented by an attorney. The testimony of witnesses is transcribed by a court reporter, who later prepares a verbatim transcript of the proceedings.

Employees enter the corporate headquarters of RJR Nabisco in Atlanta after the 1988 announcement that the large tobacco and food corporation had been acquired by Kohlberg Kravis Roberts & Co. (KKR). The FTC approved the merger of the two corporations after KKR agreed to divest certain product lines that otherwise may have given KKR a monopoly in the market for those goods.

The Trade Secrets Act, which applies to all federal agencies, a number of provisions in the FTC Act, and FTC rules together protect the confidentiality of the materials submitted to the commission. While an investigation is ongoing, it is not made public unless the company files a motion or petition to quash compulsory process (such petitions are placed on the public record).

Once the staff has gathered the evidence concerning the particular act or practice in question, the staff must analyze the evidence from both a legal and economic standpoint to decide whether there is reason to believe that violations of the law have occurred and whether the commission should exercise its discretion to initiate a prosecution. The staff must decide whether to recommend that the commission address the problem on a case-by-case basis, by litigating against individual companies, or instead to initiate an industrywide rule-making proceeding.

Assuming that the practice is either not so widespread as to dictate an industrywide regulation, or because, for evidentiary, political, or budgetary reasons, it is necessary to proceed against only one or a few respondents, the staff drafts a complaint and a memorandum supporting its recommendation that outlines the results of the investigation. If the appropriate bureau or regional director agrees with the staff's recommendation and approves the draft complaint, it goes to the commission for consideration.

Generally, the attorney advisers to the commissioners review the materials and make recommendations to their commissioner about what action the commission should take. At the same time, respondents often take the opportunity to submit written memorandums stating why a complaint should not be issued and may even seek to speak to the commissioners individually about the matter.

In deciding whether to litigate a case, the staff, the bureau director, and the commissioners inevitably must determine whether there are enough attorneys on the staff to prosecute the case. As Commissioner Andrew Strenio, Jr., pointed out in November 1988, the FTC has fewer staffers than at any time since fiscal year 1961. The regulated industries have expanded greatly since then. For example, corporations spent $1.7 billion on advertising in 1961, in contrast to $14.7 billion in 1988. Fewer and fewer staff members inevitably means fewer and fewer cases and certainly fewer large, sophisticated cases that must be handled by several experienced and savvy attorneys.

Consent Agreements

If the staff decides that a violation has occurred, the violator may be given an opportunity to agree to a consent order, which is, in effect, a voluntary agreement not to violate the law in the future. A consent order may, depending on the circumstances, contain an agreement to provide consumer redress, such as refunds, corrective advertising, or other payments in order to end the FTC proceeding. In return, the alleged violator, known as the respondent, may not have to admit that it has violated the law and saves the cost and unfavorable publicity of defending against a lengthy administrative lawsuit. If the respondent agrees to a consent agreement, the negotiated terms of the agreement are presented to the commission along with a draft complaint and a staff memorandum outlining the evidence. The commission may accept or reject the consent settlement. If accepted, the complaint, the consent agreement, and a press release announcing and briefly explaining the settlement are issued by the FTC. In addition, the agreement and the explanation are published in the *Federal Register*, the U.S. government's official compilation of notices issued by federal agencies.

After a period of 60 days, within which the commission may receive public comments on the agreement, the order becomes final unless the commission

The FTC publishes its trade regulations and consent orders in the Federal Register, *the U.S. government's official compilation of notices issued by federal agencies and of proclamations and executive orders issued by the president.*

withdraws its acceptance of the agreement. The order resulting from the consent agreement has the force of law as it applies to the respondent. However, other companies cannot rely on its terms as being binding on the FTC in its dealings with them, and others who might wish to sue the respondent cannot rely on the facts alleged in the complaint that accompanies the consent agreement as having been proved as they would be in a case that was fully litigated.

(continued on page 86)

Dream Away?
Fat Chance!

Frauds involving weight loss products present one of the most widespread problems encountered by the FTC's Division of Advertising Practices. The diet industry affects a large segment of society: 25 percent of American adults are obese, and 18 percent diet constantly. In all, there are 65 million dieters in the United States. In 1989, the advertising and marketing of weight loss products generated sales of $33 billion, a figure that is expected to nearly double by 1994.

In the early 1980s, Nutri Marketing, a mail order company, began promoting a product called Dream Away, a diet pill that the company claimed would burn away fat while its users were sleeping. According to the promotional pitch, Dream Away was made of amino acids that stimulated the release of a human growth hormone. This hormone, in turn, increased "fat mobilization" and "fat oxidation," which would lead to weight loss without special diets or exercise.

Nutri Marketing advertised Dream Away in television commercials on local and cable stations nationwide, instructing viewers to order by mail or to call a toll-free number. The U.S. Postal Service filed an administrative complaint against Nutri Marketing, charging it with using false representations to obtain money through the mails. A cease and desist order was issued against the owners of the company in June 1986, directing them to stop representing that Dream Away caused weight loss. Later, the California and Minnesota attorneys general acted to halt the deceptive practices associated with the sale of Dream Away in their states.

In May 1987, a staff attorney in the FTC's San Francisco regional office videotaped an Advanced Dream Away commercial. An FTC staff attorney in Washington also located a videotaped advertisement for Advanced Dream Away in the FTC records that was taped in March 1986. (The FTC's Division of Advertising Practices routinely videotapes hours of television programming and monitors advertisements for possible violations of FTC standards.) The attorney in Washington subsequently placed two orders for Advanced Dream Away by calling the toll-free telephone number provided in the television ad.

In January 1988, FTC attorneys filed a complaint for an injunction and a motion for a temporary restraining order with an asset freeze in a U. S. District Court in Arizona. The FTC's complaint cited several statements made in Nutri Marketing's television ads and promotional materials that the commission believed misled consumers. The FTC charged that the Dream Away tablets simply added a modest amount to the amino acids that were already present in abundance in the average American diet and that the product did not cause weight loss during sleep or in a short period of time. Based upon the opinion of a medical school professor who had conducted obesity research for 25 years, the FTC also maintained that the product neither caused weight loss without dieting or exercising nor enhanced the weight loss effects of dieting or exercising.

The court issued a temporary restraining order to put an immediate stop `to the advertising claims. In addition, it found that there was a substantial likelihood that, absent the asset freeze, the owners of Nutri Marketing would conceal, dissipate, or divert their assets so that the government could not assure that money would be available for consumer redress. The court froze the assets of Nutri Marketing's owners, effectively placing the FTC in control of their bank accounts, cars, houses, and other assets.

After the restraining order was issued, the FTC and the owners of Nutri Marketing negotiated a settlement under which the company agreed to pay $1.1 million to be used by the FTC to refund money to consumers who bought Dream Away and Advanced Dream Away. The company agreed that it would not misrepresent the performance, efficacy, or safety of any food, drug, or device and that it would not make any such representations unless it had a reasonable basis to substantiate the claim. Nutri Marketing also

A bottle of Advanced Dream Away.

agreed not to represent that Dream Away, Advanced Dream Away, or any other comparable amino acid product causes or substantially contributes to a loss of weight. Finally, the company agreed to disclose prominently in any future ads for weight control products, programs, or services that dieting and exercise is required in order to lose weight.

The FTC reimbursed $102,000 to 3,000 purchasers who had filed valid claims with the commission, and it sent checks in the amount of $19.95 (the price of a bottle of Dream Away) to approximately 47,000 customers on Nutri Marketing's customer list. The remainder of the money was donated to institutions that conduct obesity research.

(*continued from page 83*)

Injunctions

If the staff decides that a potential respondent is violating a law administered by the FTC and that quick action is necessary, it may recommend that the commission use its authority under Section 13(b) of the FTC Act to go to federal court to seek a preliminary injunction pending completion of administrative proceedings and, if the circumstances warrant, a permanent injunction and other equitable relief such as redress for consumers.

The FTC staff is likely to seek an injunction in cases in which the potential respondent might dissipate its assets, consummate a pending acquisition, or take some other action prejudicial to the FTC's ability to obtain consumer redress or to prevent an unlawful merger. The court may impose a temporary restraining order or preliminary injunction if such action would be in the public interest. The courts are also empowered to order other measures, such as the rescission of an acquisition of a company pending an administrative determination of the legality of the challenged merger, the freezing of the assets of the defendant, or the notification of potentially injured consumers. For example, in 1989 Vaughn Management was charged with falsely telling consumers they would receive an "award" at no cost, when in fact consumers had to pay a "processing fee" in order to receive their awards, and with failing to tell consumers who paid the processing fee that they had to spend hundreds of dollars more to use the airfare vouchers they received as awards. A federal district court issued a temporary restraining order that halted the misrepresentations and also froze the defendants' assets so they later would be able to provide consumer redress such as refunds.

The preliminary injunction has become the foundation of the FTC's consumer fraud program, and it has been used regularly to prevent mergers and acquisitions that seemed imminent. The FTC has also used the Section 13(b) remedies to challenge unfair and deceptive practices in connection with the offering and sale of rare coins, artworks, precious stones, oil and gas partnerships, travel services, time-sharing vacation plans, franchises, prefabricated housing, loans, and photocopy supplies.

Litigation Before an Administrative Law Judge

If an investigation persuades the FTC staff that a violation of the law has occurred and that the FTC should take action, the staff forwards the draft complaint and a memorandum in support of it, after it is reviewed by the bureau

During a hearing on a complaint brought by the FTC, James P. Timony, an administrative law judge (ALJ) (right background), listens to a witness (right foreground) answering a question posed by an FTC attorney. ALJs are employees of the Office of Personnel Management and are assigned to particular agencies, including the FTC, to hear and decide cases adjudicated by their respective agency.

director, to the commissioners. The commission holds a closed meeting in which members of the FTC staff, known as complaint counsel, appear to explain the reasons why the complaint should be issued and to answer any questions. If the commission votes to issue the complaint, it is made public and announced in a press release. The chief administrative law judge then assigns one of the FTC's three ALJs to preside over the case.

The ALJs are not FTC employees but are employed by the federal government through the Office of Personnel Management. They are assigned to a particular agency to hear and decide cases presented under the agency's rules of practice. The ALJs are charged with the responsibility of performing fact-finding functions in matters that have entered adjudication after a formal complaint has been issued by the commission. If neither complaint counsel nor the respondents appeal the ALJ's initial decision to the commission, it becomes the decision of the commission in the case. The responsibility for conducting rule-making proceedings, formerly handled by FTC employees known as presiding officers, also has been given to the ALJs.

Once a complaint has been issued, the respondent has an opportunity to admit or deny the allegations of the complaint by filing an answer. The parties then each file a nonbinding statement setting forth their theory of the case, the issues to be tried, and what they expect their evidence to prove. At a subsequent scheduling conference, the ALJ will set a schedule for hearings and for what lawyers call "discovery."

The purpose of discovery is to disclose the evidence to be presented by each side at trial in order to promote a possible settlement or, at least, to prepare for trial. Lawyers prepare interrogatories (written questions for the other side), file requests for production of documents, and conduct depositions (hearings in which potential witnesses are asked questions under oath). Each side sends requests for admissions to the other side in the hope that they can agree that certain facts are undisputed and do not need to be proved at trial.

The ALJ presides over evidentiary hearings, which are conducted much like a trial in federal court. Following the trial, both sides file proposed findings of fact, conclusions of law, and a proposed order. Based on the record, the ALJ writes an initial decision that includes findings of fact, conclusions of law, and a recommended order. If neither side appeals, the ALJ's decision and order become the commission's order unless the commission, on its own initiative, decides to review the case. If an appeal from the initial decision is filed or if the commission decides to review it, the commission accepts briefs from both sides and holds an oral argument. The commissioners have the same power to consider all the evidence as if they were rendering the initial decision. The commission may adopt, change, or reverse the initial decision, and it may request additional information from and ask questions of either side. If a final cease and desist order is entered by the commission, it may be appealed by a respondent to any U.S. Court of Appeals having jurisdiction over an area where the challenged conduct allegedly occurred or over where the respondent resides or does business or to the U.S. Court of Appeals for the District of Columbia Circuit.

Trade Regulation Rules

Both the FTC Act and the Magnuson-Moss Warranty-FTC Improvement Act of 1975, which amended the FTC Act, authorize the FTC to promulgate rules of industrywide scope. In the mid-1970s, the FTC embarked on an aggressive program of rule-making to fulfill its mandate under the Magnuson-Moss Act. Because these regulatory proceedings threatened to change the way many

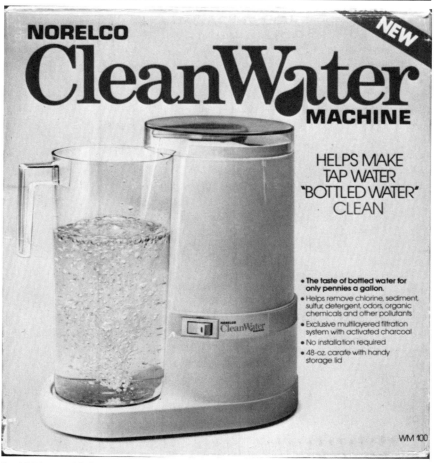

In 1988, an ALJ ruled that Norelco falsely advertised that its Clean Water Machine would make tap water cleaner even after the company had discovered that the machine added a potentially hazardous chemical to the water. The ALJ ordered the company not to misrepresent the performance of the Clean Water Machine or any other consumer appliance. The decisions and orders of ALJs are final unless an appeal is filed or the FTC commissioners decide to review the case.

U.S. companies could do business, they provoked a backlash from the affected businesses and their representatives in Congress. Only a few actually resulted in final rules, and others became bogged down in endless procedural challenges that slowed the progress of the proceedings. Many of the rule-making proceedings that started with such fanfare in the 1970s were quietly buried by Chairman Miller and his allies in the 1980s.

One of the first industrywide rule-making proceedings to go forward under the Magnuson-Moss Act focused on alleged unfair and deceptive practices in mobile-home sales and service. In 1974, four major mobile-home manufacturers agreed to enter into consent agreements that required them to implement procedures that would assure that their warranties would be performed by mobile-home dealers or the manufacturers themselves. The manufacturers decided to enter into the consent agreements rather than litigate the allegations that they had failed to honor the promises made in their warranties. At the same time, the FTC issued its initial notice of a proposed trade regulation rule on mobile-home sales and service that was based on the warranty performance program required by the consent orders. The manufacturers that entered into the consent agreements understood that the programs they were undertaking were soon to be the basis for the proposed rule.

Because it was one of the first Magnuson-Moss rule-making proceedings, each step of the mobile-home rule-making proceeding broke procedural ground. More than 400 motions and other pleadings were filed. Three sets of hearings were held at which the staff, industry, and consumer lawyers examined expert and lay witnesses concerning warranty practices in the industry. Surveys of consumer satisfaction and dissatisfaction were submitted by the FTC rule-making staff and the industry. Economists and state government regulators also testified.

Because of the many procedural questions that had to be decided in the absence of any precedents, the proceedings stretched over several years. Both the staff report and the presiding officer's report issued in 1980 recommended that the rule be promulgated based on their review and analysis of the 260,000-page rule-making record. The industry representatives (with the exception of some of the mobile-home dealers who objected to being solely responsible for the warranty repair bills under the manufacturers' warranties) vigorously disagreed and took their concerns to Congress. Action on the proposed rule was stalled and later complicated by the passage of the 1980 FTC Improvements Act and by the efforts of the new Reagan administration to redefine the law of deception.

Finally, in November 1986, the commission voted to terminate the rule-making proceeding, which, by that time, was vulnerable to the charge that the rule-making record assembled in the mid-1970s was stale. The commission concluded that the costs to the industry of complying with the rule outweighed the benefits to be provided to consumers who would have been assured that warranty promises would be performed. In June 1988, based on a petition to reopen the earlier proceedings that led to the four consent orders signed by mobile-home manufacturers, the commission rescinded the consent orders. The commission stated that the rescission was in the public interest in light of the FTC's November 1986 rejection of the remedies contained in the mobile-home trade regulation rule. Not surprisingly, the commission and its staff have shown very little appetite for embarking upon such ambitious industrywide proceedings ever since.

Violations of trade regulation rules may result in substantial civil penalties. Under Section 19 of the FTC Act, the FTC may seek in federal court civil penalties of up to $10,000 per day per violation if the violator acted with actual knowledge or knowledge fairly implied on the basis of objective circumstances that its action was unfair or deceptive and was a violation of the rule. The FTC has filed suit on a number of occasions, seeking civil penalties for violations of such trade regulation rules as the funeral rule (which governs disclosures and practices in the sale of funeral goods and services), the franchise rule, the mail-order rule, the used car rule, the credit practices rule, and others.

Other FTC Tools

The Magnuson-Moss Act also authorizes the FTC to seek civil penalties in federal court against a party that engages in conduct that violates the holding of an order previously issued by the FTC after a litigated proceeding so long as the violator had actual knowledge of the FTC's decision. This is an extraordinary remedy. To satisfy the constitutional requirements that a defendant be given due process of law before a penalty is imposed, the targets of such FTC lawsuits may litigate the issue of whether they had actual knowledge of the order, as well as whether they engaged in conduct that would violate the order had it been formally entered against them. To satisfy the requirement of proving that a particular firm has actual knowledge of a particular order, the FTC periodically sends copies of its orders or synopses of them to firms in affected industries.

The FTC also is empowered to gather information and issue reports. The commission monitors compliance with industry guides and rules issued prior to the change in commission practice initiated by the Magnuson-Moss Act. Finally, it issues consumer information material designed to assist businesses and consumers in complying with and understanding the laws administered by the commission.

In December 1990, two attorneys in the Bureau of Consumer Protection's Credit Practices Division discuss their litigation strategy in a credit discrimination case. Congress has provided the FTC with sufficient authority to do its job effectively, but federal budget cuts in the 1980s often left it without enough financial resources and staff to carry out its mandate fully.

SIX

Back to the Future

A few years ago, Michael J. Fox starred in a movie entitled *Back to the Future* in which he visited the past in a car that really was a time machine. He found the future (actually the present) very much as it was in the old days. In many ways, the FTC environment of the 1990s is much like the one faced by the commission in the early 1970s. In April 1989, the ABA, as it did in the fall of 1969, published the results of a study of the FTC by a panel of distinguished lawyers and others. The new ABA study sharply criticized the decline in FTC staff and resources and questioned whether the commission was vigorously playing its assigned role in a number of areas. Congress has also been critical of the FTC and has not formally reauthorized the commission since 1982. Until Chairman Janet D. Steiger took office in 1989, there was a sense among the FTC's overseers on Capitol Hill, very much like their attitude in 1969, that the FTC had been insufficiently aggressive in taming the merger mania of the 1980s as well as in rooting out consumer deception in advertising and in retail sales. The FTC seems poised for a change in direction back toward being a respected law enforcement agency. For the first time in more than a decade, the FTC is headed by a chairman who is not perceived as pushing a political agenda at the behest of the White House. Steiger has proved to be a quick study in the arcane area of antitrust law and is perceived as being tough on deceptive advertising.

Of course, the FTC of the 1990s is not operating in the same field as was the FTC of the early 1970s. Congress gave the FTC several major new tools during the 1970s, including the authority to seek injunctions halting illegal behavior and to freeze assets, to promulgate industrywide trade regulation rules, and to obtain broad consumer redress for past illegal conduct. It now has sufficient tools to do its job effectively if it has the proper resources.

In November 1989, Steiger announced three new policy goals along with her budget message to Congress. She asserted her desire to reverse the decline in FTC resources; to increase public confidence in the FTC as a vigorous law enforcement agency; to streamline and improve the review of proposed mergers; and to eliminate any "confrontational attitude between the FTC and constituencies that work with it, including the Congress, the states, the legal community, and public interest groups." In a March 1990 speech before the ABA's Section of Antitrust Law, she also voiced her intent to reverse the 50 percent decline in staff and funding that the FTC suffered during the 1980s.

The FTC's Resources

In one of her first interviews, Steiger told a reporter for *Legal Times*, a weekly newspaper for Washington lawyers, that she would attack staff morale problems by reallocating staff resources to improve efficiency and productivity. She added that she would seek an additional 100 jobs and $8.5 million in the next year to "bring the agency back up to speed." By the time she submitted the FTC's budget request for the 1991 fiscal year, however, the budget submitted requested only a five percent increase over fiscal year 1990.

Because of the substantial federal deficit, it is highly unlikely that the FTC will regain the staffing levels that it enjoyed in the 1970s. In light of the lack of additional resources, new initiatives will have to be limited to those that can be accommodated within existing resources.

The Outlook for the Bureau of Competition

The Bureau of Competition has reviewed some of the mergers that it evaluated in the 1980s to see if its judgments were correct. Now the FTC seems less likely to give merger participants the benefit of the doubt. In a fundamental sense, the nature of the antitrust questions may be changing. Mergers of two independent firms are undertaken today for reasons that did not exist when the

FTC chairman Janet D. Steiger hopes to increase public confidence in the FTC. Under her leadership, the FTC seems poised to reclaim its position as a vigorous law enforcement agency.

Sherman and Clayton acts were passed. Rather than combining to achieve efficiencies of scale, many firms combine simply to obtain benefits made available under the tax laws and in the financial markets. Bargaining over the final outcome of a merger becomes somewhat more difficult if the result has to be economically sound under the antitrust laws when the real reasons for the mergers are to minimize tax liabilities and raise money in the financial markets.

One of the major challenges facing the Bureau of Competition in the future is coping with the changes in merger enforcement that will result from the globalization of the economy. U.S. companies that hope to reap the benefits from the economic unification of the European Community (EC) in 1992 by buying an existing company in Europe will have to deal with changing rules and regulations on both sides of the Atlantic. In a sense, the future is now on this issue because in September 1990 each of the EC countries lost some of its individual authority over mergers. Large-scale mergers (those worth more than $6 billion) are now reviewed by the EC itself rather than by the antitrust enforcers in each EC nation. For the FTC staff, the impending unification of Europe means having to consider how to deal with the new European approach.

Also, Canada, one of the United States's biggest trading partners, is revising procedures under its Competition Act of 1986 and published guidelines for

95

mergers in the summer of 1990. The Canadian government's statement will affect mergers that involve Canadian operations. Also, those who wish to enter into joint operations with companies in Eastern Europe are seeking advice from the Bureau of Competition.

With more and more mergers involving foreign firms or subsidiaries, the FTC merger staff is experiencing increasing difficulties in gathering the information about foreign entities needed to make its decisions within the time limits set by the HSR Act. The foreign entities often seem to have a territorial point of view and exhibit a certain hostility to U.S. antitrust enforcement. Since U.S. laws do not apply overseas unless the foreign conduct under scrutiny sufficiently affects commerce inside the United States, the FTC may not always be able to force a company to supply needed information. Although the United States has negotiated several agreements with foreign nations that simplify the process of obtaining evidence from abroad, law enforcement officials must rely heavily on voluntary cooperation. There are antitrust agreements with Germany, Canada, Australia, and the Organization for Economic Cooperation and Development. The Bureau of Competition's international division acts as liaison to its foreign counterparts and provides advice and assistance to its colleagues in these matters. Clearly, the impact of the bureau's international antitrust lawyers will become much more visible in the future.

The Consumer Protection Programs of the Future

As the Bureau of Consumer Protection looks at its mission for the future, it is likely to find that it will be most active in combating fraud and in prosecuting advertising cases. As in the recent past, the FTC will be using preliminary injunctions coupled with temporary restraining orders, asset freezes, and consumer redress to combat fraud. In recent years, the commission has devoted a considerable percentage of its scarce consumer protection resources to the problem of fraudulent sales carried out over the telephone. But, as Barry Cutler, the director of the Bureau of Consumer Protection under Chairman Steiger, has lamented, it is like picking dandelions: Unless one gets at the roots and support structure, one cannot stop the seeds from scattering. Once the FTC acts against one telemarketer, others merely begin again in other states.

In the future, telemarketers who establish phone banks offering deals too good to be true to the public can expect a vigorous FTC program of injunctive

The director of the FTC's Los Angeles regional office and a staff attorney prepare for a press conference announcing a lawsuit against a fraudulent telemarketing operation that was selling investments in a gold mine. The storyboard illustrates the inactive mine site, the boiler room that was selling the investment, and some agency brochures discussing telemarketing and "dirt-pile" scams. One of the principal challenges for the FTC staff is to educate consumers about risks in the marketplace.

actions and a search for ways to deny them the support structures they need in order to carry out their fraud. For example, the FTC will seek to deny telemarketers the access they need to the credit card system. Also, companies that finance fraudulent activities by knowingly accepting and financing consumer contracts for worthless goods may receive some unwanted FTC attention. The FTC will look at applying the legal theories that establish joint liability and aiding and abetting to deter those who assist unscrupulous businesses.

The new chairman has announced her commitment to focus more attention on national advertising and to cooperate closely with state authorities. She will be devoting more resources to enforcement and attacking unfair or deceptive advertising practices that focus on young people and the elderly. Steiger has already announced that the staff is investigating advertising that encourages children to make "900 storyline" and "Dial-a-Santa" telephone calls. In some cases, the advertisements urge young children to bring the telephone receiver up to the television so that the sounds that are broadcast will cause a touch-tone telephone to make the call.

The FTC will continue to bring advertising cases before its ALJs in order to keep the FTC in control of the development of the law. In deference to the "dandelion theory," the FTC will pursue the producers of deceptive "infomercials," not just the purveyors of the deceptive products they advertise. Because the states have been more active in bringing advertising cases and developing guidelines for industry advertising, the commission will have to work hard to maintain the lead in setting national standards. The FTC should receive some assistance from the business community, which wants 1 rather than 50 different advertising standards. It was the business community, however, that was the driving force against the FTC's national advertising cases of the 1970s.

The FTC will concentrate its advertising enforcement dollars on false or unsubstantiated health and safety claims, claims involving alcohol and tobacco (particularly those directed at young people), health claims in food advertising, and in the new area of environmental claims. Deceptive practices in the marketing of health care products and services also will receive priority attention. The FTC is conducting investigations into false safety and efficacy claims for certain cosmetic surgery procedures and exaggerated success-rate claims made by providers of in vitro fertilization services. The FTC has already obtained an injunction against misrepresentations and a judgment for $250,000 in consumer redress against one provider of infertility services.

The commission will also continue to pursue deceptive practices in the marketing of diet products and weight-loss services. In 1989, hospital-based weight-loss centers brought in nearly $5.5 billion. The FTC will be looking at the representations made by these plans to be sure that they do not say that weight loss achieved through these plans will be permanent without evidence to substantiate the claims. The FTC will also investigate whether the franchisees and licensees of these plans marketed by national distributors have the necessary professional training and provide the medical oversight promised by their promotional materials.

As concern about global warming, air and water pollution, and garbage disposal mounts, consumers have indicated a willingness to pay more for products that do not harm the environment. The FTC will scrutinize claims by companies that their products are biodegradable, photodegradable, recyclable, not harmful to ozone, or environmentally safe to see whether those claims can be substantiated. Manufacturers of products made of plastic that carry environmental claims on their packaging, such as disposable diapers, may

McDonald's Corporation vice-president Shelby Yastrow holds the amount of paper wrappers that will replace the stacks of plastic foam boxes behind him for packing the Quarter Pounder sandwich. In November 1990, McDonald's announced that it would change its packaging due to pressure from environmental interests. As companies increase production of environmentally safe products, the FTC will scrutinize claims that the products are recyclable and environmentally safe.

99

In November 1990, Larry Ryan, originator of digital video interactive technology, inspects a silicon chip that will enable personal computers to integrate text with video, stereo sound, still photography, and animation. By striving to fulfill its mission to keep competition in commerce free and fair, the FTC will help ensure that the United States remains competitive in the world market.

receive requests for substantiating data from the FTC. Even comparative claims that one product is environmentally superior to others may be open to question. More traditional cases, such as the one brought against Campbell Soup in 1989 that challenged Campbell's claims that the low-fat and low-cholesterol content of its soup reduced the risk of heart disease, will continue to be high on the FTC's agenda.

Ahead to the Future

As the global markets and the U.S. economy develop through the 1990s and into the 21st century, the American public can expect to see many changes. Although there may be no moves afoot to combine the antitrust enforcement responsibilities of the FTC and the Department of Justice into one agency, there will be increasing pressure for the FTC to coordinate its antitrust enforcement activities with those of other nations. Perhaps the FTC will enlist the support of the State Department in negotiating additional mutual legal assistance treaties covering antitrust enforcement investigations, so that it may gain better access to the information it needs from foreign companies.

Because resources will continue to be limited, the FTC probably will look for creative ways to get its work done at no cost. In consumer protection cases, the FTC is emphasizing enforcement actions against firms that provide the support structure for fraudulent schemes, such as those who "launder" credit card slips and provide the deceptive scripts that are used in telephone "boiler rooms" to deceive customers. The FTC may begin referring more cases, such as those involving fraud, to the states for prosecution. Similarly, it may encourage state enforcement of FTC trade regulation rules. It will undoubtedly continue to increase its role as an advocate before other federal agencies and in the states so as to forestall problems and enhance solutions without having to act on its own budget.

There is some chance, given the current climate of reassessment, that the leaders at the FTC and the political leaders in Congress and the White House will decide that the megamergers of the 1980s did not increase efficiency but merely diverted needed capital into merger and acquisition costs rather than into research and development and other productive pursuits. The ability of the United States to compete against the EC and the Pacific Rim countries has become a serious economic issue that may lead to a reassessment of the economic theories that drove the mergers of the 1980s. In any event, it may come to pass that the "Little Old Lady of Pennsylvania Avenue" will once again be seen as an important weapon in the fight to keep America competitive.

Federal Trade Commission

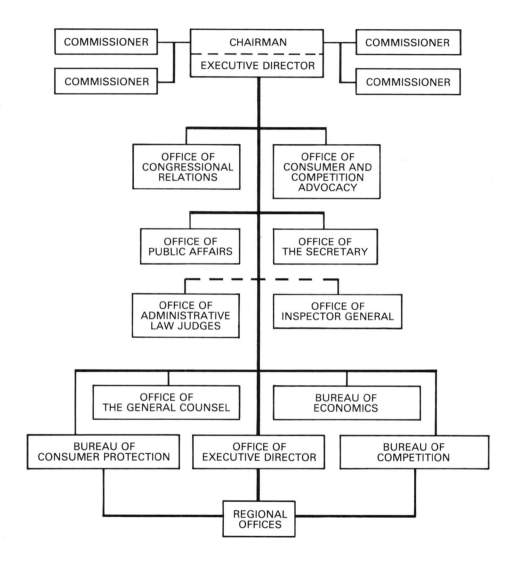

GLOSSARY

Cease and desist order   A directive issued by a regulatory agency commanding that an unlawful activity be stopped.

Clayton Antitrust Act   A law enacted in 1914 that charged the FTC with the duty of preventing and eliminating unlawful tying contracts, interlocking directorates, and corporate acquisitions and mergers.

Consent order   A voluntary agreement (settlement) between a regulatory agency and a party charged with a violation of a law that the agency administers. The charged party usually agrees to refrain from such violations in the future and to compensate injured parties.

Corporation   One of the legal forms in which a business can be established. Stockholders, the people who own a corporation, are able to act as one, and each stockholder is financially responsible only up to the amount he or she originally invested in the corporation.

Hart-Scott-Rodino Antitrust Improvements Act (HSR Act)   A law enacted in 1976 that amended the Clayton Act to require the filing of premerger notifications with the FTC and the Antitrust Division of the Department of Justice.

Horizontal restraint   An agreement among businesses competing at the same level of the distribution chain (for example, automobile manufacturers) that restricts competition.

Magnuson-Moss Warranty–FTC Improvements Act   A law enacted in 1975 that authorizes the FTC to establish standards for written warranties (guarantees) and provides consumer remedies for breach of warranty.

Merger   Any process by which two or more separate companies combine to form a single company.

Monopoly   A company that has little or no competition in its industry and controls a commodity, product, or service in a particular market. Monopolies are illegal in a free-enterprise society such as the United States.

Premerger notification   A report of an impending merger transaction that is filed with the FTC and the Department of Justice so those agencies can determine whether the proposed merger might violate federal antitrust laws.

Sherman Antitrust Act   A law enacted in 1890 that prohibits trusts and combinations that restrain trade or commerce. The FTC and the Department of Justice enforce the Sherman Act.

Trust   The consolidation of companies in the same industry for the purpose of reducing competition and fixing prices.

Tying agreements   Illegal contracts that require buyers to deal exclusively with certain sellers.

Vertical restraint   An agreement among businesses that operate at different levels of the distribution chain (for example, automobile manufacturers and dealers) that is believed to restrain trade.

SELECTED REFERENCES

American Bar Association. *Report of the American Bar Association Section of Antitrust Law Special Committee to Study the Federal Trade Commission*, September 15, 1969.

American Bar Association. *Report of the American Bar Association Section of Antitrust Law Special Committee to Study the Role of the Federal Trade Commission*, April 16, 1989.

Cox, Edward F., Robert C. Sell, and John E. Schulz. *The Nader Report on the Federal Trade Commission*. New York: Richard W. Baron, 1969.

Henderson, Gerard C. *The Federal Trade Commission: A Study in Administrative Law and Procedure*. New Haven: Yale University Press, 1924.

Link, Arthur S. *Woodrow Wilson and the Progressive Era: 1910-1917*. New York: Harper Torchbooks, 1954.

Mackay, Robert J., James C. Miller, III, and Bruce Yandle. *Public Choice and Regulation: A View from Inside the Federal Trade Commission*. Stanford, CA: Hoover Institution Press, 1987.

McCraw, Thomas K. *Prophets of Regulation*. Cambridge: Harvard University Press, 1984.

Miller, James C., III. *The Economist as Reformer: Revamping the FTC, 1981-1985*. Washington, DC: American Enterprise Institute for Public Policy Research, 1989.

Pertschuk, Michael. *Revolt Against Regulation: The Rise and Fall of the Consumer Movement*. Berkeley: University of California Press, 1982.

Stone, Alan. *Economic Regulation and the Public Interest: The Federal Trade Commission in Theory and Practice*. Ithaca: Cornell University Press, 1977.

Wagner, Susan. *The Federal Trade Commission*. New York: Praeger, 1971.

Ward, Peter C. *The Federal Trade Commission: Law, Practice and Procedure*. New York: Law Journal Seminars Press, 1989.

INDEX

PICTURE CREDITS

Pamela B. Stuart, a graduate of Mount Holyoke College and the University of Michigan Law School, was a trial attorney and deputy assistant director of the Bureau of Consumer Protection of the Federal Trade Commission from 1973 to 1979. She later served as an assistant United States attorney for the District of Columbia and as senior trial attorney in the Office of International Affairs at the U.S. Department of Justice. She is currently a member of the law firm of Lobel, Novins, Lamont & Flug in Washington, D.C.

Arthur M. Schlesinger, jr., served in the White House as special assistant to Presidents Kennedy and Johnson. He is the author of numerous acclaimed works in American history and has twice been awarded the Pulitzer Prize. He taught history at Harvard College for many years and is currently Albert Schweitzer Professor of the Humanities at the City College of New York.